THE NEWS IN TEXAS

The News in Texas

ESSAYS IN HONOR OF
THE 125TH ANNIVERSARY OF THE
TEXAS PRESS ASSOCIATION

EDITED BY WANDA GARNER CASH AND ED STERLING

THE CENTER
for American History

THE UNIVERSITY *of* TEXAS *at* AUSTIN

Contents

List of Illustrations

Foreword

DON E. CARLETON
DIRECTOR, CENTER FOR AMERICAN HISTORY

In a letter to Colonel Edward Carrington written in 1787, Thomas Jefferson famously declared that "were it left to me to decide whether we should have a government without newspapers or newspapers without a government, I should not hesitate a moment to prefer the latter."

Although Jefferson's statement about his preference for newspapers over government was an exaggeration made in support of a higher concept related to democracy, there is ample historical evidence that Texans have shared his preference in a more literal sense. For most of the state's history, Texas newspapers have been far more popular than government. A good argument also could be made that often they have been more powerful. Whatever one's views may be on the subject, there is no doubt that newspapers have had a tremendous influence on the historical development of the Lone Star State.

This historical influence is among the reasons why the University of Texas at Austin's Center for American History (CAH) has long been involved in the preservation of the state's newspapers. As every student of Texas history knows, newspaper sources often serve as the necessary starting point for research on almost any topic. When used critically, they can provide factual background, chronology, and context. And there is nothing quite like the newspaper for conveying a sense of change over time or for providing a window through which we can watch a past culture unfold page by page before our eyes. Accordingly, the center has made a special effort to acquire, preserve, and make available for research U.S. newspaper sources in every format, including hard copy and microfilm.

With 2,500 individual newspaper titles in its holdings, the center has the largest collection of Texas newspapers in existence. As manager of the Texas phase of the National Endowment for the Humanities–funded U.S. Newspaper Project, the CAH inventoried and microfilmed more than one million pages of historically valuable local newspapers, many of which were in imminent danger of permanent loss. It also has gathered an extensive collection of the papers of individuals and organizations that have played important roles in the history of the press. Included in this treasure trove of Texas newspaper history is the archive of the Texas Press Association, which has played a key role in the development of the newspaper industry in our state.

The official slogan of the Texas Press Association (TPA) is a precise declaration that the association has been "serving Texas newspapers since 1880." The essays in *The News in Texas* provide ample evidence of this service. The Center for American History is proud to be the home of the TPA archives, and we are delighted to publish these essays celebrating TPA's history.

My sincere thanks to TPA president Wanda Garner Cash, executive director Micheal Hodges, and director of member services Ed Sterling for making this book possible. I also want to acknowledge David Dettmer and Suzanne Loy of the CAH, designer Teresa Wingfield, and copy editor Kip Keller for the hard and skillful work they contributed in the effort to get this book into print.

Overview

ED STERLING AND WANDA GARNER CASH

The purpose of this book is to tell the story of the roots, progress, and dynamic effect of the Texas Press Association in the rambunctious and mettle-testing atmosphere of the Lone Star State. The book will focus on how individual newspaper publishers from disparate backgrounds have come together under the tent of their own trade association and worked collectively to develop an informed electorate, promote business, advance the public good, and improve the quality of life of all Texans. The association currently reports 508 member newspapers.

This book is intended to fill a hole in Texas history where there should be a detailed account of the role of this association of editors and publishers from weekly, semiweekly, and small daily newspapers in the development of the state. As a natural outgrowth of their membership in the Texas Press Association, newspapermen and newspaperwomen essentially become family with their counterparts from cattle ranches and grasslands, cotton country, the oil patch, mineral troves, farmlands, citrus groves, and wilderness areas. The percolation of entrepreneurial synergies and the resulting actions made possible by their gathering at an annual convention began in 1880. This fraternity has been a catalyst in the progress and development of Texas ever since.

The story of the Texas Press Association is also one of modernization through technological advances: "pony mail" and the telegraph gave way to the telephone; single-sheet presses and labor-intensive typography gave way to Linotypes and Babcock presses, then to cold type and web presses. Royal and Underwood typewriters and stuffy darkrooms were abandoned in favor of computers and cell phones.

The Texas Press Association and its members lay a major claim to helping forge the myth of the independent Texan and reveling in the reality of it. The group's sweat equity in the state was readily seen in the drive to build the

San Jacinto Monument, the construction of the state highway system, and the rallying of public opinion that brought about the designation and creation of Big Bend National Park. In 1936, at the nadir of the Great Depression, the press association took a leading role in the Texas Centennial celebration, working hard to convince the world that the citizens of Texas themselves are the heart of something unique and grand in scope.

State leaders recognize the Texas Press Association's ability to influence public policy, mobilize voters, and keep Texans up-to-date on critical issues, from water and soil conservation to food rationing and scrap collection drives during World War II. Citizens and public servants find insight and guidance on the editorial pages of community newspapers.

Even when newspapers take an unpopular stand on an issue, private citizens know their newspaper is on the job, reporting on items of interest to the community and serving as both watchdog and gadfly. In the masthead of most member newspapers is a small Texas Press Association logo. Readers learn that the logo symbolizes the fact that their newspaper is in pursuit of excellence in service to the community. They also come to understand that Texas Press Association aids its members on open-government and business issues and serves as their advocate in the halls of the state capitol. The press association, in concert with the Texas Daily Newspaper Association, fields a legislative advisory committee that scrutinizes legislation.

The story of the Texas Press Association, furthermore, is the story of family and group ownership. Many families hold tight to newspapers founded by their pioneer ancestors, and in the twenty-first century, as in the twentieth, families buy out existing newspapers and establish new ones. From the Roberts family in the Texas Panhandle and South Plains to the Hartman and Walls families on the Gulf Coast, dozens of Texas newspapers have thrived under family ownership for generations. Corporate groups such as Harte-Hanks, the Hearst Corporation, Cox Communications, and Westward Communications have shepherded significant holdings of newspapers for decades.

Despite strong and independent family and group ownership, the road to success and, indeed, survival is not and never has been a cakewalk for Texas newspapers. Thriving towns and their newspapers dry up after interstate highways are routed around them. The arrival of Wal-Mart in Texas communities takes a grievous toll as the retail giant drives out Main Street businesses. Environmental regulations and the wildly fluctuating price of newsprint and equipment makes back-shop printing presses increasingly rare, and new, regional printing presses absorb an increasing share of the presswork. Newspapers, in response to consumer demand, warm to the idea of paid online content to supplement their traditional print products.

The Texas Press Association and its members live in the crucible of all that defines the Lone Star State. From its establishment in 1880 until the present day, the association and its members have served as watchdogs of freedom and agents of change in their communities, interpreting the key issues and events of our state on their front pages.

Newspapers chronicle Texas history one issue at a time, reflecting and shaping the state's independent character. In this anthology, the personal reflections of the essayists enhance that chronicle.

Introduction

GRIFF SINGER

Given the popularity of all of the new media and communication technology, it would be logical to ask whether the tried-and-true newspaper is still relevant. It is, primarily because of such bodies as the Texas Press Association.

This book examines the background of Texas newspapers and their grand place in history and coincides with the 125th anniversary of the Texas Press Association.

The TPA now is primarily an organization of newspapers that serve the smaller communities in Texas's 254 counties. It had a tough time getting started. Some editors, conducting their businesses out of a cigar box, said finding the $2 for annual dues was tough. But the organization has prevailed, serving the people of Texas as well as the newspaper industry.

Regardless of the size of the community they serve, newspapers have long been the driving force behind getting out the news, getting things done, and getting things corrected for Texans. Newspapers still are main sources of history and information about our communities.

Michael Blackman notes later that community journalism "shaped us, steeled us, pointed us, gave us wing, and reined us in."

Texas's editors, journalists, and their newspapers were trailblazers in numerous ways. They have traveled far since the first newspaper, *Gaceta de Texas*, was launched in 1813. Texas newspapers often took the first step with new technology.

Texas newspapers made use of the newfangled telegraph service after it arrived in the early 1850s. For the first time, news of the world did not have to come by mail toted on horseback or rail. Texas newspapers also have a long association with the Associated Press. The AP hit Texas sometime about 1884, after being founded in New York City in 1848. It's doubtful that those money-saving big-city publishers who organized the wire service dreamed it would one day be the world's largest news-gathering organization.

Community newspapers in Texas were the first in the country to make widespread use of offset printing, combining that process into centralized printing facilities. They were the first to make widespread use of "cold" type, abandoning the long-serving Linotype machines and their hot slugs of metal.

Much of the credit for the change in technology and the concept of centralized printing facilities goes to the late Staley McBrayer of Fort Worth, an owner of North Texas community newspapers who in the mid-1950s pioneered the development of an affordable web-offset newspaper printing press, the Vanguard, that met the needs of smaller publications.

When the personal computer arrived on the scene, community newspapers jumped at the opportunity to take advantage of that technology. Although slow to initiate the use of costly pagination systems—lower labor costs offset the price of expensive computer software—community newspapers are now often even with or ahead of the major metropolitan newspapers when it comes to technology. Virtually all have taken advantage of the Internet and can now deliver news and advertising worldwide.

Newspapers from the beginning have shown their interest in fighting for their communities, for what is right. In fact, some have even been involved in fisticuffs: community newspapers personify personal journalism. An often-told story relates how a Panhandle sheriff, displeased at the editorial comments in the weekly paper, showed up at the newspaper office. Discussion led to a fistfight and brawl involving the sheriff and the editor, right there in the newspaper office.

Most fighting is done with words, as when newspapers press governmental officers and agencies to provide information the public has a right to know, or when they support or oppose some project facing the community. Most fight for economic development as well because advertising revenues keep newspapers solvent.

Generally, newspapers tend to stay close to home with their concerns. But at least twice during TPA's existence newspapers from across the state banded together in common cause. During the Great Depression, Texas newspapers were credited with helping successfully stage the Texas Centennial Exposition in Dallas. It was a combined effort to blend business with patriotism, as *Newsweek* described it. Centennial editions of newspapers brought in badly needed revenue, and the centennial itself helped draw investment capital from afar while introducing Texas to businesses and people unfamiliar with the state. As Patrick Cox notes in this book, the centennial helped redefine the state's character and its institutional memory.

More important in the eyes of journalists was the concerted effort to gain access to government information in Texas. Texas newspapers played a significant role in gaining legislation to create the first Open Meetings Act and the Open Records Act in 1973. The time was right: a scandal had struck at the heart of the banking industry, its lobbyists, and high-ranking state officials two years earlier. Voters were angry and embarrassed about what was going on in the state capital. The speaker of the house went to jail, and the lieutenant governor was ousted after one term. And at last, Texas had a semblance of laws dealing with public information and records, after similar legislation had been passed at the federal level and by many other states.

The Texas Press Association and the Texas Daily Newspaper Association received most of the credit for ensuring passage of legislation to open the doors of state and local government activities. Meeting behind closed doors, at secret locations, or at unannounced times by county commissioners, school boards, or city councils—as well as state bodies—would no longer be allowed or tolerated by law. The TPA and the press in general today maintain a vigil against efforts in most sessions of the legislature to restrict access to government at all levels.

All of the foregoing may paint a very serious picture of Texas journalism. But that's not the whole truth. Texas newspapers boast of a cadre of top-flight humor writers. As Jack Loftis, editor emeritus of the *Houston Chronicle*, notes, humorous prose "is perhaps the best defense available to counter the totally incorrect charge that newspapers are only interested in gloom and doom 'because they sell papers.'"

Some of us grew up reading columns from the likes of the late Morris Frank and Paul Crume. But a later generation has been taught to laugh at life—and sometimes to deal with serious issues—by John Kelso, Leon Hale, Mickey Herskowitz, Blackie Sherrod, and Molly Ivins. But look at some smaller newspapers and you'll find humor in very brief takes, often countering life's personal tribulations. Regardless, these efforts draw readers like bees to honey.

Although much progress has been noted in Texas community journalism, some changes have come slowly, for example, greater opportunities for women in running our state's newspapers.

With World War II, women became more than bookkeepers or society writers. When the men went off to war, the women left behind had to assume new responsibilities. Newsrooms have not been the same since.

However, women have been less likely to attain the position of editor or publisher, and women hold those key spots at lower percentages than they fill executive positions in other industries.

But take heart. The Texas Press Association had back-to-back women presidents in 2004 and 2005. That's a first.

As far back as the TPA convention in 1893, Julia Truitt Bishop of Austin discussed the role of women in journalism: "While women are, perhaps, not practical enough to meet the demands of modern newspapers, they have brought to those newspapers something they sadly needed—a touch of heartfelt tenderness to the hard utilitarianism of the age."

Looking at the content of today's newspapers, where the news is more featurized and stories on virtually every topic are visible, Mrs. Bishop was right on target.

Newspapers in Texas have served their communities well. If an area needs a new hospital, they are in there pitching. If reform is needed in government, newspapers are there to point out the problems and talk to people with solutions.

As Mike Blackman points out, Texas is different, primarily because from the beginning, newspapers "recorded the whole shebang: the good, bad, and prickly-pear ugly."

He also points out, "We are what we read. And for that you may thank your local newspaper as well as its loyal and sustaining companion, the Texas Press Association."

May the TPA mark its 250th anniversary.

S. GRIFFIN (GRIFF) SINGER *spent almost fifty years involved in Texas journalism, working as a reporter, editor, and teacher. His first job was on the twice-weekly* Arlington Citizen-Journal. *He was a reporter and assistant city editor at the* Dallas Morning News *and an assistant managing editor at the* San Antonio Light.

Singer joined the journalism faculty of the University of Texas at Austin in 1967 and recently retired as a senior lecturer. During the summer months for over seventeen years he worked as an assistant metro editor and writing coach at the Houston Chronicle. *He has conducted numerous workshops and programs for the TPA and the Texas Associated Press Managing Editors Association.*

THE NEWS IN TEXAS

CHAPTER 1

The Texas Press Association Helps Newspapers Make History

ED STERLING

The Texas Press Association was founded as a business and social fraternity for newspaper owners and editors in 1880, more than fifty years after printing presses produced the state's first newspapers. Texas newspapermen and -women had long recognized a need for an organization from which they could learn better ways to manage business affairs. Charter members knew that a statewide association could help them improve their product, secure community footholds, and establish permanent franchises.

Press associations in states senior to Texas's, such as Arkansas and Missouri, served as models. Members of those associations saw that quality newspapers attracted settlers and created infrastructure upon which communities could prosper. Although Texas newspapers' economic position was tenuous and threats to their survival abounded, the people who operated them held among themselves an entrepreneurial spirit. The potential economic benefits of association membership outweighed the risk of hazards in travel to meetings and the monetary cost of membership.

Three attempts to form a state press organization failed before the founding of the Texas Press Association. The earliest documented attempt occurred when the editor of the *Jefferson Herald* urged newspaper owners and editors to meet at Marshall, Texas, on June 9, 1853. One editor questioned whether Whigs and Democrats ought to associate at all, let alone meet as members of a professional association.[1] This association lived and died in the first decade of Texas statehood, leaving few details as to its proceedings.

In the following year, R. W. Loughery, editor of the *Texas Republican* in Marshall, wrote in his February 18, 1854, edition:

The magnetic telegraph is at length in operation between Marshall and New Orleans. We are no longer cut off from the balance of the world by low water and slow mails. But in the twinkling of an eye—less time than it takes to talk about it—a dispatch can be sent and received from the most distant portions of the Union where this wonder-working machine is in operation.

This breakthrough in communications technology appeared to signal something big for newspapers everywhere, but the journalistic trade in Texas suffered a setback on the heels of the introduction of telegraphy. The Civil War began, and journalists and printers left their presses to fight. Ink and paper became scarce. While in recovery from the ravages of war, Texas journalists made a second attempt to organize in 1869. A small group formed the Texas Editorial Association. Meetings were few, and that association soon disappeared. In 1873, a third group of Texas newspaper publishers met in Sherman, Texas, and organized the Texas Editorial and Press Association, a fraternity that met only four times before it died like its predecessors. Though its minutes are lost, Colonel F. B. Baillio, editor of the *Cleburne Review*, knew enough about that association to report that its demise could be attributed to the physical distance that separated members and that poor transportation facilities made meeting difficult.[2]

F. B. Baillio, Texas Press Association president in 1896–1897, described conditions confronting early Texas publishers, and the historical value of newspapers, in this way:

> There were no railroads, no telegraph lines, no electric lights, no trolley and interurban lines, no reapers and mowers, no threshing machines, no steam plows, no horseless carriages, when the printing press came to Texas; but their comings, along with recital of other things that make interesting reading, are chronicled in the files of the newspapers of the state. It may be said that you can't write history from newspapers, but the historian who neglects the files of the public press will miss a great deal of valuable information and material which can be found nowhere else.[3]

In contrast to earlier days, travel conditions in the last two decades of the nineteenth century had improved enough to facilitate the formation of a permanent press association. The dredging of bayous made waterways navigable by steamboat and mule-drawn barge. Bridges replaced rope-and-raft ferries. Steamboats and horse-drawn buggies provided means by which many representatives of the press made the journey to the first meeting of the Texas Press Association, while those who could took advantage of railroad lines that had begun to spread across the state. Even so, travel by the most modern of means presented challenges. To get to the second TPA convention in Houston, Eli T. Merriman, publisher of the *Corpus Christi Caller*, traveled via the Tex-Mex railroad line to Laredo. From Laredo he rode to San Antonio over the International and Great Northern Railroad, and there switched to the Sunset Route that brought him to his final destination.[4] This was a two-day, 500-mile rail journey. It likely would have taken a week or more for Merriman to travel the 200 miles from Corpus Christi to Houston either overland by horse or by boat through the port of Galveston.

The first meeting of the Texas Press Association took place on May 19, 1880, when seventy-seven journalists gathered at Hutchins House, a popular, twenty-year-old hotel near the banks of Buffalo Bayou in Houston. How these journalists were summoned to converge in that city and at that time is not recorded, but the result was certain: they responded to the summons and founded an association intended to enhance the quality of newspapers and "elevate the standard of living of those who produce them."[5]

On the porch of Hutchins House the founders brushed soot and dust from their clothing, then moved to the parlor and convened. They chose officers and laid the framework of the association, realizing once and for all that they could learn from one another and that they needed one another to survive and prosper. A debate ensued over the question of who should be eligible for membership, the owner or the editor of a newspaper. The decision was made to allow both owners and editors to join. Next, the founders elected J. W. Fishburn, publisher of the *Mexia Ledger*, as president. He served from 1880 to 1881.[6]

Organizational problems consumed much time during annual meetings from 1880 to 1890. At each meeting, bylaws were revised to take care of new problems. Advertising rates posed one such problem. Many attempts were made to establish a standard basis for advertising rates. At the third meeting in 1882, members defeated a resolution requiring their newspapers to charge no more for "foreign" advertising than for "home" advertising. The assembly also defeated a resolution requiring publishers to charge not less than seven and one-half cents a column inch for advertising.

Histories of the association, written in 1913 by F. B. Baillio and in 1929 by James H. Lowry, concur that debate over the question of who should be qualified for membership almost resulted in the death of the association at its first meeting. Agreement was reached by admitting both newspaper proprietors and editors who were not proprietors, but the latter were not entitled to vote on matters involving expenditures by proprietors. Commercial printers were not allowed to hold membership.

At the first meeting, membership dues were set at two dollars a year and the cost of the convention program at two dollars. Even at those amounts, members had a hard time paying. The April 25, 1882, secretary's report of TPA's third annual meeting reveals that many editors were financially embarrassed and did not pay their dues. Only about 75 members were held in good standing, against 111 the previous year.[7]

Early conventions featured lavish meals and tours and entertainment provided at a nominal charge or gratis by host cities. At the third convention, a resolution to stop further acceptance of such gratuities failed. The reason for killing the resolution was that under existing circumstances adoption of such a measure was "not necessary." However, the secretary's minutes show that a majority of the members present had failed to pay their two-dollar annual dues that year. Lack of cash did not dampen postconvention festivities, as attendees were invited to take an all-expenses-paid rail excursion to San Francisco, courtesy of railroad magnate Leland Stanford. A detailed account of this excursion was written by Jacob Moore Frazier of the *Morgan Sentinel* and published in his 1936 autobiography, *Tallow to Television.*

After 1882, TPA members continued to accept the hospitality of railroads. They enjoyed such rail destinations as New Orleans, Denver, St. Louis, and Mammoth Caves, Kentucky. In 1894, an attempt was made to eliminate discussion of upcoming excursions from the business sessions because they distracted attention from business items. It was resolved that no excursions be taken for the next two years. But the resolution was ignored: following the meeting, a number of publishers boarded an excursion train to Asbury Park, New Jersey.

The next year, members accepted junkets to Houston to attend the Confederate reunion and an international excursion to Mexico City. In 1898, a great many members took advantage of a free rail pass to Eureka Springs, Arkansas. Although storms had washed out the tracks near the White River in Arkansas, the excursionists crossed the washout and piled onto handcars. They pumped the final six miles to Eureka Springs, where they participated in a joint meeting with the Arkansas and Missouri press associations. Perhaps the most notable excursion came decades later. In 1936, TPA members traveled to Washington, D.C., on a special Pullman charter to promote the Texas Centennial and State Fair. Attendees were treated to a state dinner at the White House.

In 1886, at the seventh meeting of the press association, a motion to prohibit discussion or reference to political matters was adopted, indicating that just as in 1853, partisanship was hard for members to set aside. At conventions, breeches in decorum were not uncommon because of it. Apparently, however, this partisanship-squelching resolution had no teeth. In his history

The 1908 meeting of the Texas Press Association in Marlin, Texas.
Photo courtesy of the Texas Press Association.

of the association, Lowry recorded that the 1886 resolution had "not been kept inviolate" since its adoption.[8]

At the fifteenth meeting, in 1896, the association voted to reduce membership dues from two dollars to one dollar a year and to increase the initiation fee from five dollars to ten dollars.

In his history, Baillio contemplated a Texas Press Association with statewide reach. He speculated on the power of an association in which enough people shared a vision and were willing to work together on goals. "If publishers will agree on a thing, and act in concert, they can accomplish anything they undertake," he wrote.[9]

Baillio recognized the TPA's role in helping member newspapers overcome local hardships and, second, acting as a trusted ally and advocate at the state capital. At the association's founding and through its first ten years, publishers discussed needs for better public education in Texas, a greater volume of advertising and uniform advertising rates, the adoption of technological advances, and the enactment of improved laws regarding libel and legal publication. Brittle, paperbound copies of convention programs from the 1880s and 1890s reveal topics of discussion that would be familiar to today's newspaper managers. In those days, the most skilled editors and publishers were called upon to give programs on news reporting, advertising, circulation building, and libel. Leaders of the association called upon rank-and-file members to speak about advertising sales techniques and methods for acquiring and retaining subscribers. As Lowry wryly observed, "The average editor can speak as well on one subject as another, and the mere fact that he does not know anything about the subject assigned him does not preclude his expatiating learnedly and eloquently thereon."

While in their home offices, members of the Texas Press Association marked their lives in volume and issue numbers. Convention attendance was another way to mark time. Beyond the confines of their communities, the struggles, victories, and failures of editors and publishers—not always apparent to the communities they serve—are detailed in the proceedings of annual statewide press conventions and in TPA bulletins and periodicals. These records serve as evidence of the association's desire to stay current, meet the needs of members, and facilitate professional fellowship in a non-competitive setting.

EDWARD A. STERLING *is director of member services for the Texas Press Association. Following two enlistments in the U.S. Coast Guard (1978–1986), he entered the newspaper business as a reporter at the* Canyon News. *He later was employed by the* Tulia Herald, Amarillo Globe-News, *and* Alpine Avalanche.

NOTES

1. Ferdinand B. Baillio, *The History of the Texas Press Association* (Dallas: Southwestern Printing Co., 1916), 23.

2. Ibid., 25.

3. Ibid., 67.

4. Ida May Segrest Decker, "Eli T. Merriman—A Biography" (master's thesis, Texas College of Arts and Industries [Kingsville], May 19, 1942).

5. James H. Lowry, *Golden Jubilee History of the Texas Press Association* (Dallas-Richardson: Harben-Spotts, 1929), 111.

6. Patrick Cox, "Texas Press Association," in *The Handbook of Texas Online*, http://www.tsha.utexas.edu/handbook/online/articles/view/TT/eat2.html

7. Lowry, *Golden Jubilee History*, 117.

8. Ibid., 119.

9. Baillio, *Texas Press Association*, 28.

Chapter 2

Texas Telegraph and Register

MIKE COX

Gail Borden did not stay in Texas long enough to become a charter member of the Texas Press Association, but without the newspaper he founded, a case could be made that there might not have been a TPA—not to mention Texas as we know it.

A New Yorker who grew up in Indiana, Borden came to Texas in 1829, five years after his brother, Thomas, arrived as one of *empresario* Stephen F. Austin's colonists. Borden did not have much formal education, but he learned by reading and doing. He and his brother worked as surveyors, and as a friend of Austin's he eventually became the equivalent of a tax collector in the provisional government of Texas.

Though Borden had experience as a militia captain before coming to Texas, he knew nothing about the newspaper business. But he did understand that Texas needed a voice. Since the brief appearance of the *Gaceta de Texas* in 1813, only nine newspapers had been published in Texas. Just one sheet, the *Texas Republican*, enjoyed any significant circulation when Borden decided to venture into publishing in 1835.

With a New York–made R. Hoe and Company medium handpress purchased in Cincinnati, the Borden brothers and partner Joseph Baker printed their first issue on October 10, 1835, at San Felipe de Austin, the town established by the man who was its namesake. The firm of Baker and Borden had intended to call their newspaper the *Telegraph and Texas Planter*—a nod toward the importance of agriculture in early Texas—but the building crisis with the Mexican national government inspired them to replace "Planter" with "Register."

On page two of the eight-page inaugural issue, Borden explained: "We shall . . . endeavor to make our paper what its title indicates, the organ by which the most important news is communicated to the people, and a faithful register of passing events."

With support from the influential Austin, the *Telegraph and Texas Register* quickly became the most widely read and most authoritative paper in Texas. In a little more than two months, as the official voice of the revolutionary government, the *Telegraph* claimed a circulation of 500.

The press, Borden opined in his November 7 issue, was among "the greatest and most important inventions of man" if used to improve and enlighten the world, but if employed otherwise, "it is productive of the greatest evil." Expanding on that philosophy the following week, Borden wrote: "The columns of the *Telegraph* are at all times open to the free and impartial discussion of political subjects but can never stoop to low and scurrilous abuse of private character."

With a revolution under way, Borden had no shortage of political matters to fill his pages. The newspaper went on to play a critical part in the revolution that had begun in Gonzales nine days prior to its first appearance. But true to his philosophy, Borden did not fan the flames of that fight. Instead, he and his partners did something even more important: they printed the facts as best they could, opting to let the people make their own decisions based on those facts.

"It has never been the object of this paper to forestall public opinion, and to crowd upon the people our *own* views in a matter so important as that touching a change of government," Borden editorialized less than a fortnight before fifty-nine Texans signed a Declaration of Independence. "We have endeavored to present facts, and the publication of public documents, believing that a community composed of Americans would draw just conclusions, and act correctly when in possession of all the evidence."

Another contribution by the *Telegraph* toward Texas independence was as a medium of communication for the revolutionary government, and through it, the military. Other than word of mouth or written correspondence, a newspaper was the only source of communication in the struggling province.

On February 20, 1836, the newspaper communicated a significant development: General Antonio López de Santa Anna was on his way to Texas with thousands of troops. He had promised, the Bordens reported, "to leave nothing of us but the recollection that we once existed."

Beyond its communication role, the newspaper preserved history. On the order of the provisional government, the Bordens printed many public documents, including 1,000 copies of a handbill containing the text of William B. Travis's last letter from the Alamo, which Santa Anna had besieged on February 28. Enough copies of the handbill made it through the revolution to preserve Travis's words for posterity.

Word reached San Felipe on March 17 that the Alamo had fallen. The *Texas*

Republic of Texas–era newspaper publisher Gail Borden, circa 1865.
From Prints and Photographs Collection, Center for American History, The University of Texas at Austin. CN number 00827 a, b.

Republican having suspended publication, the *Telegraph* was the first newspaper to report the grim news that Santa Anna had overrun the old mission and killed every defender. The provisional government and its citizens soon undertook a general flight eastward, the Mexican army not far behind. The Bordens remained for the time being, reporting more details of the Alamo fight in their March 24 edition.

Three days later, realizing they were the only source of information left, they departed San Felipe, assisted in getting their press and type cases across the Brazos by the military. From the east side of the rain-swollen river, Borden watched San Felipe—and his print shop—go up in smoke as the Texas rear guard put the village to the torch.

The Bordens set up shop in Harrisburg, on Buffalo Bayou, and started setting type for another issue. "We promise the public of our beloved country that our press will never cease its operations 'til our silence shall announce to them that there is no more in Texas a resting place for a free press nor for the government of their choice," Borden wrote in the April 14, 1836, issue.

He well understood the importance of a newspaper in a revolutionary movement, and so did Santa Anna and his general officers. Only six copies of the *Telegraph* had been printed before Mexican soldiers burst into the office and seized the press.

Grabbing what they had printed, the Bordens managed to escape by boat for Galveston, where the government had gathered. The soldiers burned the town and sank the press and all the type in Brays Bayou. A week later, Sam Houston's army defeated Santa Anna at San Jacinto, but Borden had no press to tell the story with.

A myth developed that Borden recovered the sunken press and used it again later, but that was not the case. As historian Marilyn Sibley later wrote, if the resourceful Bordens could have saved the printing equipment, they would have done so.

Three men who had come to Texas hoping to join the fight soon had a major impact on the *Telegraph*. Jacob and James Cruger along with a one-armed doctor named Francis Moore Jr. had traveled from Ohio with a group of volunteers called the Buckeye Rangers. Arriving too late to participate in the rout at San Jacinto, the trio nevertheless joined the army.

Newly elected President Houston furloughed most of the army in September 1836, leaving the Cruger brothers looking for a job. Moore stayed on as an assistant surgeon, but with the revolution over, he did not have much to do. After a brief stint as a merchant, Jacob Cruger took a job with the *Telegraph*.

In July, with a new press purchased on credit in New Orleans, the Bordens relocated to the republic's new capital, Columbia, a small town on the west bank of the Brazos. With the first session of Congress set to convene there that fall, the first issue of the *Telegraph* in its new location was published August 2.

Cruger must have conveyed a sense of business optimism about the *Telegraph*, because Moore purchased an interest in the newspaper on March 9, 1837. Just shy of two months later, the new partnership published their first issue in Houston, the city's first newspaper. Only a few months later, on June 20, Jacob Cruger bought out Borden, who left Texas and went on to invent canned milk. The new publishers brought out their first edition as joint owners on June 24, noting that the firm of Borden and Moore had been "dissolved by mutual consent."

During a twenty-month period, Borden had produced seventy-four editions, chronicling some of the most important events in Texas history. Borden's biographer, Texas historian Dr. Joe B. Frantz, summed up the pioneer newspaper publisher's philosophy in twelve words: "He believed in a free press, but also in a free public."

The new owners of the *Telegraph* would be somewhat more partisan in their stewardship. Cruger oversaw the production of the newspaper while Moore ran the editorial side. The good doctor could not cure all the evils of society, but he tried. He editorialized against the various vices, particularly drinking and gaming, and decried violence in editorial blasts at dueling and gun fighting.

The editor also advanced his political position, often writing disdainfully of President Sam Houston and his government. That led to Houston to say of Moore, who had lost an arm in his youth, "The lying scribbler of the Telegraph, is a one armed man. You never would forgive me for abusing a cripple, but I must confess that one arm can write more malicious falsehoods than any man with two arms I ever saw."[1]

The firm of Cruger and Moore extended their reach on April 8, 1839, with the publication of Texas's first daily newspaper, the *Morning Star*. When the republic's capital moved from Houston to the newly created city of Austin in 1839, Jacob Cruger went with it to start a newspaper called the *Texas Centinel* (so spelled), first published on January 15, 1840.

Though no longer in Houston, he retained his interested in the weekly *Telegraph*, which Moore continued to run. The Crugers and Moore now owned what loosely could be called Texas's first newspaper chain. (They shut down the Austin newspaper in 1842 when the seat of government temporarily returned to Houston.)

The *Telegraph* had been a voice of reason during the revolution. But Moore felt no reluctance in urging history-changing ideas. He crusaded for nine years for Texas's annexation to the United States, a change that finally took place in 1846.

Five years later, Cruger sold out to Moore, who discontinued publication of the *Morning Star*. Moore kept the *Telegraph* for another three years before selling it in 1854 to Harvey H. Allen, younger brother of the two brothers who founded Houston, Augustus C. and John K. Allen.

Neither Moore nor Cruger, the two men who had institutionalized the *Telegraph*, survived the Civil War. Moore left Texas for the North, where he died in 1864 in an accident. Cruger chose to fight for the South, dying of illness while serving in the Confederate army.

But their old newspaper lived on. Allen converted the weekly to a triweekly on April 30, 1855, but apparently was not as good an editor as his brothers were city builders. He sold the newspaper to a stock company in 1856.

The new owners picked Edward H. Cushing to run their newly acquired sheet. For the first time since Moore had enlivened its columns, the *Telegraph* began clicking again. Offering Texans a mixture of news and opinion,

Cushing returned the newspaper to prominence. He eventually bought out the owners, becoming the sole proprietor.

Rag paper may have been hard to come by during the war, but not news. Though he sometimes had to use wallpaper and even gift wrap to print his newspaper, Cushing kept Texas informed of state and national developments, publishing numerous extras. On February 6, 1864, he turned the newspaper into a daily, noting casually in that edition, "Our paper being to all intents and purposes a daily, we have thought best to call it so."

The *Daily Telegraph* not only survived the war, but also continued to grow in readership during the bloody fraternal conflict, its circulation nearly quadrupling. Subscribers had to pay twenty dollars for six months, but that was in Confederate money, a currency worth considerably less than Yankee dollars.

When the war ended, Cushing went north to buy better production equipment. Back in Texas, he expanded the newspaper and advised his die-hard readers that the Lost Cause was indeed lost. He said they should get on with their lives and support the newly reunited United States. As one writer later put it, "His position was too far in advance of public sentiment to meet popular approval."[2]

Not caring for his politics, "certain gentlemen of means" formed a syndicate to buy the newspaper. Setting what he thought was a ridiculously high price of $30,000 in gold, Cushing was startled when the group agreed to meet his demand. Having been made an offer he could not refuse, Cushing sold the *Telegraph*.

Under the anonymous new owners, the paper lost ground in the market. In over their heads, the investors unloaded the *Telegraph* on W. J. Hutchins, who in 1867 sold it to William G. Webb. The new owner ran the newspaper until the fall of 1873, when he suspended publication—the first time since the end of the revolution that the *Telegraph* was silent.

After a hiatus of a few months, the *Telegraph* reappeared as a morning newspaper in March 1874 under the ownership of Allen C. Gray, whose parents had come from Virginia to Galveston in 1838. Gray put together a good staff, and soon the *Telegraph* had more circulation than any other Houston newspaper. But the nation, and Texas, still was trying to recover from a near economic depression that had begun in 1873. That, and a protracted rainy spell that left the streets a bog and "prostrated business" in Houston, seriously affected the newspaper's bottom line. Pressured by creditors, Gray suspended publication on February 11, 1877.

Though this time the *Telegraph* got no change of batteries, by then Texas had roughly 130 weekly and daily newspapers. Gray stayed in the printing business as owner of Gray-Dillaye and Co. in Houston.

When the Texas Press Association had its organizational meeting in 1880 at the Hutchins House in the Bayou City, Gray attended. In fact, he got appointed to a five-man committee to draft a bill on public printing and have it ready in time for the next session of the legislature.

In another link between Gail Borden, the TPA, and modern Texas journalism, his grandson, Gail Borden Johnson, founded an afternoon newspaper in Houston in 1878 called the *Post*. Despite several changes in ownership and one brief publication lapse, the newspaper survived until 1995.

Part of the *Post* story is related in another way to the newspaper Borden founded and the early members of the TPA. The *Telegraph*'s last proprietor, Gray, went on to write the first history of Texas newspapers. His work, "History of the Texas Press," was included in Dudley G. Wooten's *Comprehensive History of Texas*, a book published in 1897. By that time, the TPA had become an important advocate for Texas publishers in issues that would continue into the twenty-first century, from libel to legal notices to open records.

"The press of Texas," Gray opined, "has, from its inception in 1829 to the present day, been worthy of the country and the people it has represented. In every respect it will compare favorably with that of the older States, and few countries, indeed, can present an array of editors such as Texas may point to with justifiable pride."

Gail Borden and the *Texas Telegraph and Register* had set the standard.

MIKE COX *began his newspaper career in 1965 as a "tape boy" and high-school news columnist at the* Austin American-Statesman. *He went on to spend nearly twenty years as a journalist, working for the* San Angelo Standard-Times, *the* Lubbock Avalanche-Journal, *and again at the Austin newspaper, where he closed out that part of his career in 1985. An elected member of the Texas Institute of Letters and the author of twelve books, he currently is communications manager for the Texas Department of Transportation.*

NOTES

1. Clement, *Books on the Frontier*, 65.
2. Gray, "History of the Texas Press, 399.

BIBLIOGRAPHY

Baillio, F. B., Henry Edwards, and A. B. Norton. *A History of the Texas Press.* Dallas: Southwestern Printing Company, 1916.

Clement, Richard W. *Books on the Frontier: Print Culture in the American West, 1763–1875.* Washington, D.C.: Library of Congress, 2003.

Frantz, Joe B. *Gail Borden: Dairyman to a Nation.* Norman: Univ. of Oklahoma Press, 1951.

Gray, A. C. [Allen Charles]. "History of the Texas Press," in *A Comprehensive History of Texas*, edited by Dudley Wooten. Dallas, 1896.

New Handbook of Texas, s.v. "Gray, Allen Charles," 3:292. Born October 4, 1830, in Fredericksburg, Virginia, Gray was a printer for the Confederate government during the Civil War and during Reconstruction helped Governor Richard Coke in organizing a state printing operation. In addition to writing a history of Texas newspapers, Gray edited his father's diary, published as *From Virginia to Texas, 1835: Diary of Col. Wm. F. Gray*. He died in Houston on June 11, 1913, leaving a wife and three children.

Sibley, Marilyn McAdams. *Lone Stars and State Gazettes: Texas Newspapers before the Civil War*. College Station: Texas A&M University Press, 1983.

CHAPTER 3

The 1936 Texas Centennial

NEWSPAPER PROMOTIONS AND
THE CREATION OF THE "TEXAS EMPIRE"

PATRICK L. COX

The centennial celebration of Texas's independence provided a stimulus that significantly altered the state's economic and cultural history. The one-hundred-year milestone produced celebrations throughout the state that garnered widespread participation and national recognition: through the festivities, Texas established a definitive image that would set itself apart from its neighbors in the Old South. Texas newspaper publishers provided much of the vision and stimulus for the event, intended as a launching point that would move the state out of the economic doldrums of the Great Depression. As *Editor & Publisher* reported in June 1936, "far greater than the temporary benefits, loom the benefits that far-sighted newspapermen envision for years to come." *Dallas Morning News* publisher George B. Dealey avowed, "Texas in 1936 will be discovered for the first time by the people of the United States."[1]

As *Business Week* described the centennial celebrations for 1936, the festivities were a blend of "patriotism and business." Promoters intended to attract outside capital, visitors, and the attention of those individuals and businesses unfamiliar with the Lone Star State. The exposition spread far beyond the fairgrounds in Dallas to become an exercise in redefining the state's character and its institutional memory. In a state still absorbed with its southern ties and its allegiances to the Lost Cause myths of the Confederacy, the state's newspaper publishers proved to be a driving force in the creation and promotion of centennial events with a distinct Texas flavor. In fact, Texas would often come to be described not only as a unique part of American history, but as an "empire" unto itself.[2]

The Texas Centennial joined four other major expositions of American history, knowledge, and commercial enterprise during the years of the Great Depression: the Century of Progress in Chicago (1933), the Panama-California

International Exposition in San Diego (1935), the Golden Gate International Exposition in San Francisco (1937), and the New York World's Fair (1939). In contrast to these affairs, the 1936 centennial of Texas independence served as a pivotal event in the manifestation of Texas's culture and accomplishments. Largely from the efforts of the state press, both daily and weekly, the centennial's themes and images left indelible impressions on the public for generations to come. This chapter will focus on the large centennial exhibits and promotions in Dallas and Fort Worth.

Texas declared its independence from Mexico in 1836. After a series of disasters at the Alamo and Goliad and a long retreat, a force led by Sam Houston defeated Santa Anna, the president of Mexico and the leader of its army, at San Jacinto on April 21, 1836. The Republic of Texas existed for nearly a decade prior to its annexation into the United States. The infant republic endured and awaited admission into the United States as the nation debated over the extension of slavery and the admission of slave and free states. The state's revolutionary heritage, along with its colonial and Native American history, suddenly ascended in the 1930s as a rival to the celebration of the Confederate past.

How this spirited image of Texas's past became part of the collective memory of the state and the nation derived from the centennial celebrations of the 1930s. As John Bodnar explained about public memory in the United States, collective ideas originate from "a political discussion that involves not so much specific economic or moral problems but rather fundamental issues about the entire existence of society: its organization, structure of power, and the very meaning of its past and present."

The Texas Centennial occurred during one of the most economically trying times in the nation's history. Many civic leaders joined with the newspaper publishers to extol the financial benefits of these large-scale celebrations. For the future of the state, the era transcended the collective memory of the era into a new dimension and interpretation of regional history. "Texanism," the rise of Texas heritage and identification, assumed a new mantle of importance. The beliefs, symbols, stories, language, images, and physical structures that encompassed this new public memory originated in this centennial era. Furthermore, the image of Texas as a distinct region apart from the Old South gained its impetus during this period in the public sphere. Much of this improvised cultural heritage (that maintains a presence to this day) originated with the ideas and promotions of the publishers of Texas daily newspapers.[3]

The Texas Press Association aided in the formation of the first Texas Centennial Survey Committee to plan and finance a statewide celebration.

Beginning in 1924, Lowry Martin, the advertising manager of the *Corsicana Daily Sun*, served as the workhorse of the centennial movement. A central part of Martin's strategy included winning unstinting support from the Texas newspaper industry and the endorsement of the state's political establishment. Editorials and articles appeared throughout the state. From the very outset, Lowry and other early promoters called for a massive celebration, similar to the large expositions held in other states.

During the years of planning, Jesse Jones served on the statewide coordinating committee. But his tenure was marked by uncertainties of the scope of the centennial celebration. Jones's business and political activities also distracted him. Though he maintained reservations about the feasibility of one primary exposition site modeled after the world's fairs of the early twentieth century, Jones saw the benefit of historical themes and messages as an essential component of centennial events. The onset of the Depression and his appointment to the Reconstruction Finance Corporation (RFC) brought an end to his leadership on the Centennial Commission, but Jones was to play a role in financing many centennial-related projects during the 1930s.[4]

Lowry Martin and the Texas Press Association kept the centennial celebration effort alive after Jones's departure from the board in 1930. Martin provided an ongoing stream of information, surveys, and promotions to newspapers. As economic conditions worsened throughout the state, the concept of a statewide commemoration of its birthday began to gain momentum. Many civic and political leaders viewed a centennial celebration as a potential stimulus to revive the flagging economy. The campaign resulted in a constitutional amendment passed by the state legislature and submitted to the voters during the November 1932 general election. Nearly three out of four newspapers in the state supported the proposal. The amendment, which called for a celebration combined with an unspecified commitment for funding by the state, passed during the same election that Texans overwhelmingly voted for Franklin Roosevelt and John Nance Garner.[5]

Houston's civic and political leaders believed that the competition for the main exposition came down to a battle between Houston and Dallas. If the selection involved only historic considerations, Houston would be a natural choice because of its role in Texas independence and the early Republic. "But that equation is entirely eliminated by the centennial law," the *Houston Post* editors wrote. "It is now simply a matter of which city makes the highest bid."[6]

A state commission selected Dallas as the location for the official exposition. Not to be outdone, Houston, San Antonio, and Fort Worth scheduled their own celebrations. Neighboring Fort Worth created the Texas Frontier

President Franklin Delano Roosevelt speaks at the Cotton Bowl during the Texas Centennial Exposition. *Photo courtesy the Franklin D. Roosevelt Presidential Library.*

Centennial and "The Winning of the West." San Antonio and Houston hosted events to commemorate battles of the Texas Revolution. The newly completed San Jacinto Monument and Historical Museum near Houston opened on the anniversary of Sam Houston's victory over Santa Anna's army in April 1836. Numerous events throughout the state extended the celebration to nearly every county. Huntsville, Sam Houston's hometown, featured the initial sale of the Texas Centennial postage stamp. Stamford held a cowboy reunion and roundup. Crystal City hosted a spinach festival and proclaimed Popeye as honorary mayor. Every major daily in the state published a special centennial edition, sometimes totaling more than one hundred pages, stocked with history, anecdotes, and ads.[7]

Centennial editions, similar to anniversary and other special commemorative publications, served newspapers and the larger community. These highly publicized newspapers validated the publication as the official collector and interpreter of historical memory. Centennial publications enhanced the role of the newspaper as a cultural authority and opened the door for other businesses and individuals to enlist in the narrative effort. Editorial content and the selection of the historical articles remained the prerogative of the editorial staff. The presentation was nearly as important as the content of these commemorative issues. Large, eye-catching print, artwork, photos, and other illustrations formed an essential part of the grand exposition that unfolded throughout these extensive editions.

Newspaper publishers and other civic leaders selected and promoted commemorative events for many reasons. Major celebrations rallied popular support and quieted anxiety about change. The centennial celebration provided a platform to promote exemplary citizen behavior and corporate responsibility to the larger community. The special editions of newspapers and the centennial promotions clearly supported each of these virtues. Anxiety over the ongoing economic depression maintained its hold over the population, and one of the stated goals of centennial proponents included a celebration that would improve the collective outlook of the citizenry. As evidenced by the intense competition among the large cities for the coveted centennial headquarters, widespread support from the major urban communities existed. In the promotions of all these celebrations, proponents urged citizens to participate and extol the virtues of a past built on traditional American ideas—independence, liberty, freedom of expression, and the desire to establish a better society.[8]

As the leading proponents of the centennial, the state's major newspaper publishers reaffirmed their position in the center of cultural and political leadership. They recognized that their individual positions as community leaders, along with their role as newspaper publishers, depended on the success of these types of activities. In addition, this success depended on the continuation of the daily newspaper as the focal point of communication in the community. As the centennial events gained acceptance and achieved regional and national recognition, the newspapers and their publishers reached the apex of approval by the citizenry. In April 1936, a large contingency of Texas newspaper owners and editors took an eleven-day, seventeen-state tour with Governor James Allred to promote the event to the nation.[9]

As Texas prepared to celebrate the anniversary of its independence with centennial activities across the state, promoters looked to Washington and to Austin for public dollars. The state and federal governments each provided $3 million to kick off the events. Local communities also sold bonds to finance the construction of new projects. To prime the pump with more dollars, Washington provided money for many of the buildings and Centennial projects that provided thousands of jobs for Texans. Rejecting traditional southern suspicions of utilizing federal dollars for improvements and services, Texas newspaper editorials largely encouraged public and private support for centennial events and improvements. The $3 million provided by the state legislature included $500,000 for advertising and promotion. When Congress allocated $3 million, Vice President John Nance Garner, a native Texan, became chair of the federal commission overseeing expenditures in the state.

Publishers also contributed to what may be termed the "Origin Myth" that took firm root in the collective memory of Texans. *Fort Worth Star-Telegram* editor J. M. North described these sentiments in a 1935 letter to *Dallas Morning News* editor Ted Dealey. "The history of Texas began 100 years ago," North stated, which conveniently ignored the entire history and role of Native Americans, Spain, Mexico, France, and the United States prior to 1835. The historical interpretation promoted and distributed during the centennial provided an explanation that accommodated the racial and economic views of the state's hierarchy.

Briefly, Texas fought for its freedom because of Spanish and Mexican misrule and oppression. These hardy Anglo-Saxon pioneers created a land of opportunity after the conquest of the native populations and the government in Mexico City. The state's business and political leaders combined forces to forge a new frontier and began promoting new communities where life would peacefully progress and where conflict would be downplayed and avoided.

These themes accommodated the prevailing racial stereotypes, class distinctions, and cultural prejudices of the era. Mexican Americans were associated with barbarism and hostility. African Americans were viewed as inferior and uncivilized. This interpretation ignored cooperative efforts and public-private cooperation in favor of private initiative. The Populists, Socialists, and adherents of other political movements outside of the mainstream were conveniently ignored. Frederick Jackson Turner's frontier thesis, which instilled patriotism and individuality, found a comfortable residence in the Lone Star State.[10]

Once chosen as the main site for the centennial events, Dallas acted as a magnet for the state's celebration. Planning and promotion for the main event occurred in Dallas. News of the event originated in Dallas through special publications and through the pages of the *Morning News* and the *Times Herald.* Newspapers throughout the state received the *Centennial News,* a weekly publication with information on the progress of the event, and *Texas Centennial Review,* a newsletter with ideas and information for local events. From the largest cities to the smallest communities in the state, the centennial emerged as the leading issue of the day. The patriotic message moved into diverse areas and populations with its unifying themes of Texas's history and its experience as a state that stands apart from the rest of the union. As the *Dallas Morning News* reported on April 1, 1935, "every progressive community in the state, it would seem, is busy" with a centennial program.[11]

The *Centennial News* provided ongoing information on centennial events, construction activities, exhibits, and promotions. The *Centennial News* gained a national circulation and served as a source of information for the print media and radio productions. In its very first edition, the lead story announced "$3,000,000 U.S. Aid in Centennial." The article announced that the federal contribution "marks the peak for federal contributions to any World's Fair to date and brings national recognition to the Texas Centennial Exposition." The first edition also declared that the "History of Texas is Theme" and "Color and Romance Background for Exposition." Describing Texas's colonial history and independence from Mexico, the article stated, "The only state in the Union once a world nation in her own right, Texas is an empire exceeding in geographical dimensions the bonds of any country in Europe." The romanticized version of the state's history and its "empire" image became common themes throughout the centennial year and served as a mainstay in publications for many years.[12]

The *Centennial News* highlighted select events, but failed to cover the behind-the-scenes battle for the premier exhibition site. The selection of Dallas embarrassed and frustrated major daily newspaper publishers in Fort Worth, Houston, and San Antonio. Amon Carter, the *Star-Telegram*, and Fort Worth civic leaders moved to close the gap created after Dallas received the winning bid as the host city for the Centennial. As Fort Worth's civic leaders sought state funds for their own celebration, the *Star-Telegram* moved to quench some of the fires that still burned from the competition for the centennial celebration. The *Star-Telegram* and the *Morning News,* which often threw barbs at each other through their editorial pages, realized the Centennial expositions offered a potential economic boom in the midst of the Depression. "We can't conceive of people coming to see the Livestock Centennial and not seeing the main Centennial at Dallas," *Star-Telegram* editor J. M. North wrote to Ted Dealey of the *Morning News*. "We believe that two attractions will supplement and benefit each other and that neither can possibly be hurt by the other."[13]

In spite of the rivalries between the major urban publishers, *Editor & Publisher* magazine noted that the centennial promotions were a boon to newspaper businesses in the state. Though the promotions immediately yielded increased employment, more advertising, and a jump in the tourist trade, greater benefits would accumulate in subsequent years. "The more people who visit Texas and see its wonders and get acquainted with its citizens, the more people will invest their capital and their lives in Texas, according to the shrewd judgment of Texas publishers," the article stated. George Dealey immodestly predicted that the exposition would create "more development and greater posterity in the state of Texas than have the last

25 years." Amon Carter, *Fort Worth Star-Telegram* publisher, Tom Gooch, editor of the *Dallas Times Herald*, James Pollock, business manager of the *Fort Worth Press*, and *Houston Press* business manager John Payne joined in the rosy predictions. For emphasis, the article included a cartoon of a cowboy wearing a large western hat with "Texas" on the brim and a basket over a candle that proclaimed "Texas Billion Power Candle Light."[14]

Texas newspapers saw increased circulation and advertising revenue from the centennial. Retail stores that used to buy 5,000 to 20,000 lines of advertising, "but which dropped out entirely during the depression, are 'coming back to life,'" stated Clyde Melton, business manager of the *Dallas Dispatch*. Tom Gooch of the *Times Herald* said that newspaper circulation dropped in summer months, but in 1936 the publication experienced a gain in readers. At Fort Worth newspapers, advertising and circulation also increased. Building permits increased by 186 percent and retail business surged to pre-Depression levels of 1929. Houston reported similar increases. "Increased population for Texas, increased capital and increased progress are sure to result," *Dallas Morning News* publisher George Dealey predicted.[15]

With their rival expositions, Dallas and Fort Worth gained national headlines as evidence of a "major outbreak of exposition fever." The competing shows may have appeared to be a tribute to the rivalry between the two cities, but *Business Week* reasoned that both communities would enjoy the "chime of cash registers" from crowds anticipated to number in the millions making their way to the two Texas cities. The article noted the substantial contribution from the federal government and the local and state contributions. It also lauded the success of the celebrations in attracting large corporations such as the major automakers, each of which constructed its own multimillion-dollar structure at the Dallas fairgrounds.

The *Dallas Morning News* attempted to downplay the rivalry. In a July 15, 1936, editorial, the *News* stated, "In the Frontier Centennial our neighbor to the West preserves the tradition of the Old West in the spirit of the jazz age." The "highly publicized notion" of the competition between the Dallas and Fort Worth exhibitions was a "press agent's dream. It has no real bearing on the success of either the Centennial Central Exposition in Dallas or the Frontier Centennial in Fort Worth."[16]

Centennial funds provided construction and landscaping for Fair Park in Dallas. Construction provided much-needed jobs, but labor strikes by Dallas building-trades union members slowed down construction. The state contributed over $1 million, and the federal government contributed $1.5 million and funded more than fifty Dallas mural projects as part of the Public Works of Art Project. The Texas Hall of State, a million-dollar building to honor

Texas heroes, became the center of the permanent buildings. The park site included museums as well as exhibition buildings for petroleum, industry, communications, agriculture, and transportation. Centennial visitors enjoyed rides and entertainment on the midway and visited recreations of Judge Roy Bean's courtroom in the Jersey Lily Saloon and Admiral Richard Byrd's "Little America" camp in Antarctica.

President Roosevelt, hosted at a dinner by R. L. Thornton and other Dallas bankers, appeared in Dallas amidst great fanfare. The Dallas newspapers carried all the positive, promotional stories for the event. Few stories about the labor strife during the construction appeared in the pages of the dailies. The special centennial editions of the Dallas newspapers completely omitted any news of labor problems.[17]

Texas, along with its southern neighbors, maintained a strict Jim Crow atmosphere in all aspects of daily life. However, the main exposition contained the Hall of Negro Life, the first time that African Americans had received this type of recognition at a national exposition. Also, "nationally famous Negro orchestras" led by Cab Calloway and Duke Ellington appeared. African American business and community leaders worked with Centennial promoters for this landmark appearance. The *Dallas Express*, which had a history of attacking lynching, voting restrictions, and segregation, advocated for African Americans' inclusion in the state pavilion in Dallas. After the *Dallas Express* agreed to support the Dallas exposition and participate in the bond campaign, the Negro Hall of Life received $100,000 as part of the $3 million federal appropriation.

In rural and urban Texas, unemployment and poverty ran much higher in the black community than the white community. In Dallas, African Americans represented half the city's unemployed in the mid-1930s. Only one major African American business, the Excelsior Mutual Insurance Company, managed to survive to 1937. Thus the Hall of Negro Life represented a symbol of hope and accomplishment for the black community. Included in the hall were murals depicting African Americans contributing to the music, art, and religion of the nation.

The exhibit also represented a small achievement in opposition to the segregated life of the 1930s. A. Maceo Smith, the African American insurance executive, led a concerted effort to include the Hall of Negro Life at the exposition. Smith's early work with the Dallas NAACP and white business leaders established a pattern that would expand in the coming decades as the African American community began to expand its efforts to combat segregation.[18]

At the dedication of the Centennial Exposition on June 7, a host of dignitaries and thousands of visitors attended. As Sam Acheson of the *Dallas Morning News* wrote, the festivities opened "before the largest crowd ever gathered in the Southwest." An estimated 250,000 people attended, "making it the greatest occasion in the history of Dallas and the most notable event in Texas since Sam Houston and his men changed the course of the New World at San Jacinto." Extensive coverage over radio stations and in the state's newspapers heightened the enthusiasm for the great event. Governor Allred introduced Secretary of Commerce Daniel Roper. As he inserted a gold key to unlock the ceremonial gate, Roper proclaimed, "Texas welcomes the world." The years of planning and promotion paid off with the extensive national publicity the Centennial received.[19]

Secretary Roper escorted a delegation of officials that included state and local leaders and descendants of Stephen F. Austin. Later that day, Roper dedicated the Federal Building and visited the Hall of Negro Life. In his speech that evening, entitled "Texas and the Nation," Roper surprised many by praising the progress of African Americans. "No people in all history can show greater progress in their achievement in seventy-three years than the American Negro," the commerce secretary said. "This is traceable to their patient, loyal, patriotic attitude toward their country and to their gifts of soul and song." The Dallas newspapers carried the remarks as part of the coverage of the opening ceremony.

But later, the *Dallas Morning News* carried more critical stories that depicted African Americans in a less flattering light. "History of Negroes from Jungles to Now" and "black faces deep into slices of watermelon" comprised some of the uncomplimentary coverage of the Negro Hall of Life. The statements undoubtedly provided some comfort to fair organizers who had acquiesced in the demands of African Americans for construction of a separate facility.

But to make sure that no one would overlook the state's Confederate heritage, a statue representing the Confederacy stood in the center portico of the Centennial Building. Confederate leaders appeared prominently in murals in the Great Hall of State. President Franklin Roosevelt dedicated a statue of Robert E. Lee on his horse Traveller as one of the Centennial highlights. Allegiance to the Old South and Confederacy remained strong even as civic leaders elevated the Texas Lone Star alongside the Stars and Bars.[20]

Even after Dallas won the competition for the main exposition, Amon Carter pushed for a separate Centennial site for Fort Worth. Following the untimely death of the popular entertainer and newspaper columnist Will Rogers in 1935, Carter urged the construction of a memorial coliseum in honor of his longtime friend. Rejected by the Public Works Administration

(PWA), the plan was reborn in the form of a Frontier Centennial Exposition. A 135-acre tract west of downtown Fort Worth, formerly occupied by the military, became the chosen site.

The Fort Worth Frontier Centennial Exposition emerged as Amon Carter's *cause célèbre*. Carter united the Fort Worth business community behind the promotion as the western alternative to the Dallas celebration. The venue would offer the entertainment and lavish productions that Carter believed that the Dallas venue omitted. The *Fort Worth Star-Telegram* declared that Fort Worth would become the beneficiary of increased jobs and would receive favorable publicity for the city's businesses. Carter's newspaper and WBAP radio carried daily stories and promotions of the event. A series of front-page editorials in 1935 boasted of the benefits. "Fort Worth can stage a show that in appeal to visitors will equal that of any other city or the main Centennial itself at Dallas," Carter wrote. The benefits would bring "large and immediate cash-drawer returns to every businessman, professional man and property owner in Fort Worth."[21]

Carter lobbied his friends in Washington to assist with the funding. After obtaining a loan and grant from the PWA along with privately funded bonds for the multimillion-dollar project, Carter learned in early June 1936 that the funds were insufficient to complete construction. He wrote Vice President Garner, only days prior to the dedication, that the Fort Worth production needed more money. "Costs have exceeded estimates thirty to forty percent." He claimed that the project provided jobs for more than 3,000 people. "Can you not see your way clear to giving us some relief immediately?" Carter asked. "I assure you that it would be a Godsend to us."

Carter wrote to Jesse Jones, chairman of the RFC, soliciting loans up to $500,000. "There would not be a Chinaman's chance for you to lose a penny on this note," Carter stated. If Jones faced any legal problems, Carter suggested that he "would be fully justified in waiving them, as no doubt you have found necessary in many cases where you have rendered emergency financial assistance." Carter concluded that everyone would be protected in the investment and would be amazed at the "magnificent" production. "Nothing like it ever has been shown in America." Eventually, another $50,000 in federal money found its way to the Fort Worth promoters.[22]

When Carter obtained funding for the Fort Worth exposition, he and fair organizers raced to open before their Dallas neighbors. Delays forced the Fort Worth exposition to open a month after the exhibit in neighboring Dallas. Carter utilized the staff of the *Star-Telegram* and WBAP for publicity, planning, and accounting for the Fort Worth production. Prior to the official launch, Carter invited hundreds of newspaper publishers and editors to attend a preview. WBAP provided an hour-long show that was fed to network radio stations around the nation. At the July opening, news reports stated the production was "a startling blending of Texas longhorns, cowpunchers, chuck-wagon, six-pistols and naked Indians, with show girls, Billy Roseian scenic effects, Paul Whiteman's music and Sally Rand's bubbles." President Roosevelt telegrammed congratulations to Carter from the yacht *Sewana* off the coast of Nova Scotia. "Best of luck to you all," the president wrote.[23]

Governor Allred and other state political and business leaders officially launched the opening. New York director Billy Rose featured a highly antici-pated floorshow, the "Frontier Follies," at Casa Mañana. One of the attrac-tions for the show included a "chorus of some 500 beautiful girls." Rose also brought his acclaimed one-ring circus production of "Jumbo" to the theater. "The atmosphere of a Texas town of 1849 will be perfectly recreated," one account stated. "There will be soldiers, Indians, Mexicans, cowboys, wagon trains, stage coaches, buffalo, all the frontier business enterprises, such as trading posts, saloons and dance halls—all open for business."

The floor shows and the liquor attracted the crowds. According to Carter's biographer, "illegal liquor was served everywhere because Amon had made a deal with the state's Liquor Control Board. The summer heat often made the Fort Worth exposition unbearable, but throngs of people continued to appear. Critics and visitors praised the productions for months.[24]

The Texas Centennial Exposition in Dallas closed in November 1936. The Fort Worth Frontier Centennial suspended most operations by Thanksgiving. Over six million people attended the six-month long celebration in Dallas, and an estimated one million visited the Fort Worth show. Visitors included President Franklin Roosevelt, his wife Eleanor, Vice President Garner, and a host of national and federal officials. Over 350,000 schoolchildren from Texas and other states attended the Centennial celebrations.

The Dallas and Fort Worth events, especially when considered along with others around the state, expanded the national awareness of Texas. The festivities laid the foundations for a growing tourist trade. The centennial events also provided economic relief in the form of thousands of jobs and substantial improvements in many communities around the state. Finally, the celebrations offset some of the ongoing concerns about the Depression and lifted the spirits of many of the state's citizens. For newspaper publishers, the increased revenues, circulation, and recognition provided welcome relief. Publishers whose proclamations had appeared extravagant in 1935 actually achieved many of their goals.[25]

Centennial events and their promotion by the state press illustrated the desire to accept Washington's expanded presence, especially in the form of federal dollars. As long as the social and political order remained in place in the state, Texans maintained their allegiance to the traditional one-party Democratic system. Projects like the Centennial allowed Texans to boast of an individuality that, on the surface, set them apart from the rest of the South and the nation.

The New Deal projects and the expanding role of the federal government sometimes produced criticism and divisions within the business and political leadership of the state. Although some grew increasingly nervous about President Roosevelt's policies and the direction of the Democratic Party, Texas editors took solace from the knowledge that friendly Texans still commanded major positions in the legislative and executive branches. Even with their power and influence in Washington, newspaper publishers and Texans from all walks of life realized that the Depression retained its grip over the region and the nation.

Kenneth Ragsdale, author of a history of the Centennial, stated that many out-of-state visitors "expressed their praise for the 'new Texas'; they found not the countrified folks they had expected, but an 'ultramodern' culture." This changing attitude among non-Texans ultimately had a great cultural impact on the state, negating the "pride with shame" syndrome and instilling a new sense of state pride in Texas. Regional self-consciousness was, after all, not a congenital deformity. Dallas retailer and civic stalwart Stanley Marcus reflected on the impact of the Centennial in his city and the state. "I've frequently said that modern Texas history started with the celebration of the Texas Centennial, because it was in 1936 . . . that the rest of America discovered Texas. The spotlight was thrown on Texas and people from all over the United States came here."[26]

Daily newspapers showed evidence of prosperity as a result of the 1936 Centennial celebration. But the recession of 1937 hit Texas and the nation with a vengeance. The *Morning News* closed its long running *Semi-Weekly Farm News* and merged it with the daily. Dealey complained in his annual report that with the exception of WFAA, all of the divisions lost money in 1938. Dealey sold the afternoon *Dallas Journal* to Houston businessman James West. Commenting on the sale, Dealey reported that the corporation received only twenty cents on the dollar, "but we were perhaps lucky to receive anything."[27]

Even with the successful centennial promotions and revenues, publishers still faced difficulties in maintaining their newspapers as profitable enterprises during the final difficult years of the Great Depression. In 1940, George B. Dealey turned over the presidency of the News to his son Ted Dealey. The Belo Corporation's annual report disclosed that advertising rates still fell short of supporting the newspaper operation. The report stated that both the "leading newspapers" in the city, the *News* and the *Times Herald*, had lost money. However, the Dallas corporations survived, since they were "supported largely by radio revenues." Belo owned WFAA, and the rival Times Herald Corporation owned KRLD. Ted Dealey stated, "We have the modest conviction that the *Dallas News* is being managed more sanely and more wisely than is the business of our nearest rival" and that the "competitive situation will adjust itself." With this disclosure, he asserted, "we confidently anticipate that, in the long haul, we will come out 'at the top of the heap.'"[28]

Historian Dewey Grantham surmised that by the end of the 1930s, the New South formula had won the debate over the character of the southern economy. The New Deal provided a source of capital with few governmental strings attached. At the same time that regulations for industry, finance, agriculture, and labor were being put in place, some of the old walls of resistance and blame that Texans and other Southerners hurled at the rest of the nation came tumbling down. The metropolitan newspapers of the state took the lead alongside Texas politicians who formulated these fresh ideas. Continuing differences led to conflict and criticism, especially when issues involved a challenge to segregation and the labor system of the region. Although displeasure increased in the years prior to World War II, the disputes failed to completely dampen loyalties to the national Democratic leadership. Publishers retained their close connections to the federal leadership and relied on the entrenched Texas congressional delegation and their allies in the government to offset any serious challenges to the dominant coalition back home.[29]

Historians agree that the federal presence expanded in the South during the 1930's, but disagree on the extent of its impact on the region and its meaning for this generation of Americans. For many during the 1930s, especially the rural poor, African Americans, and Mexican Americans, their suffering continued and sometimes worsened. Yet life for many rural and urban dwellers, including some minorities, showed some degree of improvement. Texas and the South were not entirely agrarian. Urban communities expanded and the workforce increased, partly in response to federal initiatives. These programs, aided and abetted by the urban daily press, provided an alternative to the poor tenant farmers of the region. Although they criticized many federal programs and offered only lukewarm support for others, Texas daily-newspaper publishers acknowledged this shift in alignment and advocated the establishment of federal programs in the region. Public utilities, a minimum wage, work standards, relief programs, federal loans to business, the improvement of public education, and other New Deal programs found fertile ground and editorial support from the state's leading newspapers.

Texas publishers adhered to the consensus philosophy that had carried them forward from the early years of the twentieth century. This approach was followed in the difficult years of the 1930s, when debate finally moved from Prohibition to substantive issues of business expansion, labor and race relations, expanded public education, and improved health. The publishers also helped set a tone of race accommodation and tolerance, albeit within a segregated system. The newspapers remained opposed to federal antilynching legislation and affirmed their support of the poll tax. They steadfastly refused to carry news of accomplishments by African Americans and Mexican Americans. They tolerated the discrimination exercised in most of the New Deal programs in Texas and the rest of the South.

Yet by the 1930s, the major dailies in the state refused to enter into the vile, race-baiting tirades that many southern politicians and newspaper publishers indulged in. They endorsed many of the programs that were to provide a seedbed of expanded opportunity to all people regardless of their skin color or background. Also, the centennial established bridges of communication and cooperation between white and black business leaders in these urban communities. The differences in the racial communities remained wide, but some bridges were established through the support of the New Deal and its promise of a better life. The era marked the beginning of a period when the southern press would have to recognize the need to reshape the region's economic and social structure.

Although the financial ledgers had not returned to the levels of the boom years of the 1920s, the centennial year in Texas served as a watershed for the state's publishers. Reviewing the accomplishments of the centennial year, the editors of the *Texas Almanac* believed that the events signaled a "return of prosperity" and "served the purpose of bringing full realization that the old Texas had passed—that the centennial event meant more than the passing of a mere historic milestone."

The soil and natural resources still held great wealth for the state's citizens and businesses. After 1936, state leaders believed that expanded opportunities in the form of manufacturing would supersede agriculture and extractive industries. Texas had finally passed "into cultural and economic adulthood." The state and its citizenry never resembled an empire, but the image remained firmly implanted as an image promoted by the Texas press and other boosters. Most of those dreams of progress and economic success had not yet been realized, but the groundwork was firmly in place as a result of the centennial year and the contributions of the state's newspaper publications.[30]

PATRICK COX *is assistant director of the Center for American History at the University* *of Texas at Austin. He is the author of* Ralph W. Yarborough, the People's Senator *(University of Texas Press, 2002) and coeditor of* Profiles in Power: Twentieth-Century Texans in Washington *(new edition, University of Texas Press, 2004). He serves on the board of directors of the American Journalism Historians Association. A former newspaper editor and a cofounder of the* Wimberley View, *he is the recipient of many awards from the Texas Press Association.*

NOTES

1. "Publishers See Permanent Gains," *Editor & Publisher*, June 20, 1936; reprint in Box 15-10a, Amon G. Carter Papers, Texas Christian University (hereinafter referred to as AGCP). Portions of this article are taken from the author's manuscript "'Touching All Questions of Public Concern': Texas Daily Newspaper Publishers and the Modernization of Texas." The study focuses on the history of prominent Texas daily-newspaper publishers in the early twentieth century.

2. *Business Week*, June 6, 1936, 17 (copy from Box 15-109, AGCP).

3. John Bodnar, *Remaking America: Public Memory, Commemoration, and Patriotism in the Twentieth Century* (Princeton, N.J.: Princeton Univ. Press, 1992), 14–15.

4. Kenneth B. Ragsdale, *The Year America Discovered Texas: Centennial '36* (College Station: Texas A&M Univ. Press, 1987), 8–19. Ragsdale provides the most comprehensive study of Centennial events and activities throughout the state.

5. Ragsdale, *Centennial*, 22–29.

6. *Houston Post*, March 18, 1934.

7. *The New Handbook of Texas*, s.v. "Texas Centennial," 6:297–298. Every major daily in the state published a special centennial edition, sometimes totaling more than one hundred pages, stocked with history, anecdotes, and ads.

8. Bodnar, *Remaking America*, 15. Bodnar acknowledges many of these themes as important contributors to collective support from diverse elements of the community.

9. *Centennial News*, April 27, 1936.

10. J. M. North Jr. to Ted Dealey, July 26, 1935, 16 (Box 13, AGCP); Michael Phillips, "The Fire This Time: The Battle over Racial, Regional, and Religious Identities in Dallas, Texas, 1860–1990" (PhD dissertation, University of Texas at Austin, May 2002).

11. Ragsdale, *Centennial*, 119–121; *Dallas Morning News*, April 1, 1935.

12. Texas Centennial Exposition, September 7, 1935. Reprinted in Wallace O. Chariton, Texas Centennial: The Parade of an Empire (Plano, Tex., 1979).

13. J. M. North Jr. to Ted Dealey, July 26, 1935, 16 (Box 13, AGCP).

14. "Publishers See Permanent Gains," AGCP.

15. Ibid.

16. *Business Week*, June 6, 1936, 17 (Box 15-109, AGCP); *Dallas Morning News*, July 15, 1936.

17. *Dallas Morning News*, June 12, 1936; Patricia Evridge Hill, *Dallas: The Making of a Modern City* (Austin: Univ. of Texas Press, 1996), 118–119. The Dallas Open Shop Association, organized in 1919, opposed union activities in the city and subjected members who knowingly hired union workers to a $3,000 fine. The

local AFL leadership cooperated with businesses that resisted CIO organizers and refused to publicly condemn the violence and atrocities. (See *Nation*, October 9, 1937, "Dallas Tries Terror.") Based on the resistance to CIO organizing attempts in Dallas and other cities in the South, historian George B. Tindall concluded that the "South remained predominantly nonunion and largely antiunion" (*The Emergence of the New South, 1913–1945* [Baton Rouge: Louisiana State Univ. Press, 1967], 515, 522).

18. Ragsdale, *Centennial*, 305; *Centennial News*, April 27, 1936; Phillips, "Fire This Time," 276–280; James David Boswell, "Negro Participation in the 1936 Texas Centennial Exposition," (master's report, University of Texas at Austin, 1969), 1. Phillips described the Negro Hall of Fame as "an island of integration."

19. *Dallas Morning News*, June 7, 1936; Ragsdale, *Centennial*, 231–232.

20. *Dallas Morning News*, June 8, 20, 1936; Ragsdale, *Centennial*, 232; Phillips, "Fire This Time," 292.

21. Ragsdale, *Centennial*, 214–218; *Fort Worth Star-Telegram*, August 30, 1935, and March 25, 1936.

22. Amon G. Carter to Vice President John Nance Garner, July 23, 1936 (Box 17-10b, AGCP); Amon G. Carter to Jesse H. Jones, July 8, 1936 (Box 15-10b, AGCP); Ragsdale, *Centennial*, 210–220, 288–289.

23. Franklin D. Roosevelt to Amon Carter, July 18, 1936 (telegram in Box 17-10b, AGCP); Damon Runyon, "Gotham's Famous Flock to Texas," July 27, 1936 (clipping in Box 17-10b, AGCP).

24. "Fort Worth Frontier Centennial," *Texas Weekly*, April 11, 1936 (clipping in Box 17-10, AGCP); Flemmons, *Amon: The Life of Amon Carter, Sr., of Texas* (Austin: Jenkins, 1978), 325–326; Ragsdale, *Centennial*, 260–265, 282–283.

25. Ragsdale, *Centennial*, 294–295. Ragsdale stated that both major expositions actually lost money. Profit-and-loss figures proved to be misleading, as many of the bonds and notes for the exposition were never redeemed.

26. Ragsdale, *Centennial*, preface, 302–303.

27. "1937 Annual Report" and "1938 Annual Report," 7:8 and 7:9, A. H. Belo Archives, Dallas, Texas (hereinafter referred to as AHB).

28. "1940 Annual Report," 7:11, AHB.

29. Grantham, *The South in Modern America: A Region at Odds* (New York: HarperCollins, 1994), 167–168.

30. *Texas Almanac Supplement 1937* (Dallas: A. H. Belo Corp., 1936), 4.

CHAPTER 4

Community Newspapers Tell Us Who We Were and Who We Are

MICHAEL BLACKMAN

The historical and social heritage of Texas is recorded in the pages of its newspapers. Beginning in 1813 with the Gaceta de Texas, *newspapers in Texas have played a key role in describing events as they occurred, disseminating news, posting legal and commercial notices, and promoting or discrediting a cause. Today historic Texas newspapers serve genealogists, historians, journalists, and other researchers who seek to understand our past through recorded information.*

"The Importance of Newspapers," from the Texas Newspaper Project, sponsored by the Center for American History, University of Texas at Austin

If it weren't for all the little papers capturing the beautiful insanity called Texas, then we'd just be another Oklahoma in a big hat.

Mike Cochran, veteran Texas journalist

In Texas, community journalism found a home early.

Good for us.

Because from Texas's fledgling moments, community journalism shaped us, steeled us, pointed us, gave us wing, and reined us in.

Without it, Texas wouldn't have been the same—not its history, its culture, its hell-bent independence, its quaint and boisterous iconoclasm. Its persona.

Our persona. Think of it as supersized. Think of our image, how others see us, how we see ourselves.

Think of our icons, our idiosyncrasies, our bigs, biggests, and bests. Our passions and pride, e.g., big hair and the State Fair and Friday night football. Barbeque and longnecks, Blue Bell and Baptists. Cowboys of all varieties. Big money and big cons. Big oil, big busts. Savings and loans gone wild, and south. Big talk and big egos, big hats and big buckles. Big flags over car lots. Oh, whatever.

Face it: Texas is different. And not just because it was once itself a republic.

No, it's different because from the beginning our newspapers dutifully recorded what Texans were up to, what Texans reveled in, what made them proud, and what sometimes made them bigger than life—recorded the whole shebang: the good, bad, and prickly-pear ugly. So documented, Texans wouldn't, couldn't be the same, then or today. If we're all shaped by the dint of a history unique—better that than sun or saddle sores—one might presume the following:

We are what we read. For that, you may thank your local newspaper . . . as well as its loyal and sustaining companion, the Texas Press Association, which this year celebrates 125 years of riding herd.

Long before television, well before movies or radio or literature would portray the Texan at work and play, there was the local newspaper that defined who we were.

WHO WE ARE

As a roving Texas correspondent during his four-decade career with the Associated Press, Mike Cochran estimates he has visited more than 300 newsrooms across the state, looking for the next prototypical Texas story.

"If the large metros are the backbone of the Texas persona, it is the smaller dailies and weeklies that provide its heart and soul," says Cochran. "For 40 years I dealt with community papers on a daily basis, and I found their staffs' knowledge, enthusiasm, and sense of excitement refreshing and inspiring—and vital to giving Texas its special character.

"More than anyone, these papers define and reinforce what is typically Texas."

In fact, they do that and so much more. Always have.

If, indeed, one wishes to more fully appreciate the cultural impact of newspapers, how they contribute to our both liberating and constraining embrace of Texan-ness—Oh Lordy, where would we be without our image and icons?!—one would do well to consider a wider-angle shot of our journalistic heritage. For the record, from Texas's earliest days our newspapers captured the daily ferment of a flowering society, playing, as the professors say, "a key role in describing events as they occurred, disseminating news, posting legal and commercial notices, and promoting or discrediting a cause."

For much of this newspapering journey, the Texas Press Association has proved an indefatigable partner, an organization whose leadership has helped guide, in many cases, bald passion into a profession, and through education and advocacy has sunk deep the underpinnings of a newspaper and media profile that today stands high—a progressive, multibillion-dollar industry—indeed, is envied throughout the nation.

Our very first newspaper, *Gaceta de Texas*, in its first issue on May 25, 1813, summoned 3,000 followers at Nacogdoches to rise up and smite the Spanish, to forge a republic. Thus aroused, they went forth, and failed. *Gaceta de Texas* also petered out forthwith. But earnest efforts must count for something.

A legacy, say.

Texas's frontier editors grew up stubborn and strident, their newspapers political cudgels. More often than not, their adversaries were deemed not opponents but enemies. Skunk fights between rival papers employed name-calling and motive-impugning that sank to a tacky level nigh impossible to fathom in today's polite society, Super Bowl halftimes notwithstanding. If you found a soft spot in an editor's heart, chances are it was rotten.

In those days, Lord help the politician held in editorial disfavor. For instance, the *Austin Statesman* in 1871 listed these reasons for rejecting one congressional candidate:

He is good for nothing. He is an infinitesimally small quantity—less than zero. He don't know on which side of any question to vote. He is an atheist. He is an advocate of freelovism and woman's suffrage. He stole cotton from the Confederacy. He knows as much about the proper duties of a congressman as the devil does about holy water.

Clearly one must presume standards for public service were higher back then.

In the old movie westerns, unrepentant editors were always getting beat up, spit at, slapped silly, shot at just because they expounded views more oblique than conventional wisdom might approve of.

Texas has been there.

In 1862 a discontented reader shot to death E. Junius Foster, editor of the *Sherman Patriot*, because of Foster's support for the Union cause; the upset reader's sentiment was not then uncommon in the upper tier of North Texas counties. Adolph Douai in the 1850s had to sell his paper, the *San Antonio Zeitung*, after readers abandoned their support and businesses pulled their ads. Douai, a prominent member of Texas's German community, incited disfavor by penning fervent antislavery editorials, a position embraced by many of Texas's German immigrants in the years leading up to the Civil War.

(Not all editor dustups were so rooted in political ideology. For instance, a county judge killed the editor of the *Waco Tribune* in 1897 for not printing his letter. Flat blew away J. W. Harris and his brother, W. A. The letter to the editor lent support to William Cowper Brann, the fiery editor of the Waco journal the *Iconoclast*. A few months later Brann himself was shot to death—shot in the back—by the father of a woman student at Baylor. Brann had frequently editorialized about what he believed to be relentless seizures of hypocrisy at the Baptist institution, in part as they related to possible lapses of female rectitude.)

Texas newspapers had an attitude, all right. Bulbous with exhortation, they helped shape our state constitution into what it is today, at heart the 1876 model and the legal instrument that governs us all. OK, a scary thought, wags suggest. But that's why God made amendments, which festoon our sacred document with good intentions and vested interests.

In 1880, a day of promise dawned for Texas newspapers. Over the horizon rode the Texas Press Association, if not to the rescue, certainly to the betterment of roughly 280 newspapers then publishing in Texas, most of them weeklies.

In Houston that year seventy-seven editors and publishers met to conjoin their common interests for the good of their enterprise, their readers, their state, and their nation. In the TPA's early years it sought to standardize advertising rates, improve editorial quality, press for open government, and impress on elected officials a young state's dire needs. What better excuse to meet, eat, drink, and talk shop every year?

The TPA didn't disappoint. Its vision, moxie, and muscle have stood well time's relentless test.

So: Did it improve Texas newspapers? Did it help create a professional climate conducive to success, editorially as well as economically? Did it help promote the noblest tenets of civic responsibility?

Yew betcha, a Texan might argue, in a buncha ways.

By the early 1900s, for instance, the TPA persuaded the legislature to pass first civil libel law in Texas, helping restrain the more virulent editorial tirades. In a healthy nod to equality, the organization successfully lobbied for the establishment of an educational institution in Denton that would one day become Texas Woman's University.

When drought ravaged several South Texas counties, the TPA collected funds for the parched.

TPA members went to battle with the rest of America in World War I, mustering support wherever possible. In the 1920s, when the Ku Klux Klan was having its regrettable way with much of Texas and the South, Texas editors, often at their own peril, frequently stirred their readers with the "condemnation of lynching and anti-Klan editorials," says Patrick Cox, assistant director of the Center for American History at UT-Austin. Notably, Cox adds, these editorials were based not so much on moral outrage as on how the white-sheeted hoods "might tarnish the community . . . hurt it economically."

Highway safety, the Texas Centennial celebration, national park status for Big Bend, a monument for the San Jacinto battleground, World War II bond drives—these are just a few of the endeavors to which the Texas Press Association and its members would devote their energy and resources.

Along the way TPA members were rarely reluctant to illuminate their positions on the major stories of their time, from Prohibition to voting rights to civil rights.

"I'M JUST GLAD YOUR MOTHER ISN'T HERE TO READ IT."

Like a free puppy from the classifieds, community journalism can foster bountiful feelings of warmth and loyalty among its readers—notwithstanding an occasional little accident on the carpet.

To participate in community journalism, or even to appreciate it from a distance—say, a reader's living-room recliner—is to expose yourself to a deeply personal experience, both intellectual and emotional, often vexing and rewarding, confounding and reassuring. After all, our smaller communities harbor few secrets, and the role of community newspapers is to report that which is news in all its multiheaded definitions. For newspaper folk—from publisher to printer to carrier, reporter to advertising rep—there's no hiding behind big-metro anonymity with its security detail at every door.

You're fair game when you produce a flawed product. Amazing how fast one can cancel ads and subscriptions.

And for citizens written about, opening up the local paper can be as thrilling as reading about your daughter scoring the winning goal or as disconcerting as seeing your name in print for nonpayment of property taxes. It's all there, for all to see—your neighbors, friends, preacher, banker—and they're not talking about the winning goal.

Nothing connects quite like community journalism.

"People in small towns tend to be more influenced by what they read in a weekly or small daily," says former Speaker of the U.S. House of Representatives Jim Wright, who, as a young congressman from Weatherford, paid considerable attention to his hometown *Weatherford Democrat*. Some politicians will say that they pay more attention to smaller papers than the metros, believe them to be more important to their political careers. Wright won't go that far, but allows, "I know I always read the *Democrat* more thoroughly than the *Star-Telegram*. I just think people tend to read every word in their weekly and small daily."

Those readers, of course, include advertisers, who have on occasion been known to read their local paper from yet another highly personal perspective.

"You want to talk about pressure," says one former publisher. "Just wait till the son of your biggest local car dealer gets into some scrape with the law and daddy comes knocking on your door, wanting you to keep his name out of the paper. You've already lost a couple of other big accounts because of the economy, and now you're facing the possibility of maybe not making your next payroll."

This, too, is just part of the personal side of community journalism—relevance, readability, and making a difference—one that a car-dealing daddy may not fully appreciate.

"In small towns, the folks you write about you run into every day on the courthouse steps, and Sunday on the steps of the Methodist church," says Roy Eaton, owner-publisher of the *Wise County Messenger*. Nothing like a little homegrown familiarity to promote accountability, he says. But that's how better community newspapers like the *Messenger* not just survive but thrive. His words are instructive.

"We try to balance out the news—what we think are the most important stories for everybody. We run lots of photos from all over the county of nearly 60,000," he says. "We're based in Decatur, but we're a county paper. It's a true challenge. We have eight school districts, and our goal is to get every kid's name in the paper at least once every year."

Eaton's 7,000-paid-circulation paper, like countless other community papers across Texas, makes itself relevant and readable—the *Messenger* has won more than 100 awards for editorial excellence since Eaton took over in 1973. The paper has long pressed local government bodies—e.g., the county, the school boards—to embrace a policy of openness, and it strives constantly for creativity in its local coverage. It can't devote column after column, for instance, to a major national story like Iraq, but when the first son of Wise County came home from Iraq, Eaton noted that "we followed him all day, when he went back to his school, even when he went to see his grandmother. Ran a huge four-column picture of him on page one, and then a pictorial essay. People seemed to appreciate it."

John Dycus, the longtime journalism professor at UT-Arlington who has sent scores of students into community newspapering, offers this assessment of community versus metro newspapers: "Sometimes I think the large papers write for each other; the smaller ones, at least those successful, write for the people they're covering."

My mother loved her local weekly paper, the *Western Observer*, published in Anson, Texas. If something was in the paper, it was Bible. It was, by golly, as real and true as the preacher criticizing the devil and cheap beer at the VFW.

"Do something bad, everybody in town's gonna know," she liked to say. "Honey, I don't ever want to see your name in the paper for something you done bad. Everybody will know. And paper doesn't get it wrong."

Mamas can be so lovingly unconditional sometimes.

It was thus from that perspective that Mama didn't believe I had graduated from college in 1967, because my name failed to appear on a list of local grads in the *Observer*. My mother had attended the graduation ceremony, but son's name wasn't in her paper—*oh, where did her son go afoul?*

She called me at work that summer to tell me how disappointed she was that Baylor had decided to withhold my degree. And why hadn't I told her?

A mistake, I said, over and over. But there was no consoling. She just didn't believe me, and was in tears.

Finally, my boss at the time, Henry Holcomb, assistant managing editor of the *Baytown Sun*, told me to get my degree, get in his car. We were going to my Aunt Helen's in Houston. We would have her, my degree in hand, call her baby sister, my mother, and confirm that her only son had, indeed, graduated.

Which we did, to Mama's considerable delight—and relief.

After Mama's funeral in 1975, Dad and I found numerous clippings she had tucked away in a shoebox, more or less the full if meager history of her son in print: son hits two homeruns in one Little League game; son's Hampshire gilt gives birth to nine piglets during a farrowing party; son scores a (his only) touchdown against Merkel in 1961; son goes to FFA public-speaking contest; son graduates from high school. In that shoebox she hoarded a childhood as only a mother's love can.

It was a couple of weeks later, while with my father in the oilfield, that I confessed to getting whiskey crazy at the rodeo the night before. A couple of highway patrolmen had taken offense at some of my errant habits, and since I would be leaving to go back to New York in a few days, I didn't want him to be surprised if he saw my name in the paper in association with a little post-rodeo celebration.

We were overhauling a pump at a well site; it was whiskey-sweaty hot. He never looked up, and for the next twenty-six years of his life never mentioned the moment again. But that morning in a mesquite pasture in Jones County, he invoked the Lord's name briefly in a less than complimentary fashion and said, "I'm just glad your mother isn't here to read it. It would break her heart."

She probably would have canceled her subscription, for if it was in her local paper, it by golly had to be true.

One thing you can say about Texas community newspapers. They got spunk, in spades.

Always did. If you don't believe it, just ask Billie Sol Estes, or check the history of the Texas General Land Office and Bascom Giles. Or consult the U.S. Marines, specifically their recruiting and training policies. All figured most prominently in Pulitzer Prize–winning reports done since the mid-'50s by papers in Pecos and Cuero and Lufkin, respectively. Other small Texas dailies also captured journalism's highest national honor: papers in Alice, Amarillo, and Odessa.

In fact, as the *TPA Messenger* noted in 2003, the first four Pulitzers won by Texas papers went to small dailies; to date, Texas papers have won nineteen Pulitzers since 1955. You could say that papers in Houston, Dallas, and Fort Worth had good role models when, finally, their turn came.

In Texas, the iconography of high school football sates us all. We're all players, one way or another. You played or your kids played or the kids marched in the band or choreographed yells with the pep squad or, most likely, your life was so dreary and dull in small-town Texas that come Friday night you actually looked forward to going to the game just to get another cafeteria coffee and Frito pie. It's just a Texas thing, what we all grew up with, as Texan as driving ten miles over the speed limit and measuring distance in six-packs. And community newspapers, through singular devotion to the sport, helped propel Texas football to its vaunted station.

"For the small town, your [Friday night] football coverage is one of your most widely read newspaper sections. That's the one item everybody gets wrapped up in," says Dave Campbell, the Waco sportswriter who in 1960 founded the annual *Texas Football* magazine and is the planet's acknowledged authority. (When James Michener was researching small-town football for his epic novel *Texas*, he came to Waco to interview Campbell.)

As Campbell told me, "Small-town people are close to the coach and team, and that's to the benefit of all because it creates a chemistry between them."

And for decades, small-town dailies have capitalized on that frenzied symbiosis.

PERSONAL REFLECTIONS AND LESSON LEARNED

I once had a boss who was marvelously steeped in community journalism. Irrepressibly so. This was not my small-daily editor who carried his teeth in his back pocket and insisted on a minimum of thirty-five headlines on page one. This was the publisher of a large metro daily whose most prominent newsroom credo was this: Everybody within circulation reach should be guaranteed getting his or her name in the paper at least four times—when they are born, when they graduate from high school, when they marry, when they die.

Further, he told his newsroom staff one day, if he didn't start seeing such documentation in his favorite newspaper, heads were going to tumble. Fast.

Many of us thought his passion annoyingly excessive. Too much trouble to get births from hospitals, all of them, in a timely way. Who cares when some kid graduates in a metro area on a million-plus.

Little slow out of the blocks were we. Oh, the folly of youth.

Upon seasoned reflection, aided and abetted by roughly a half century of reading and, at times, full-flask practicing of community journalism, I now believe my old boss, himself a much-practiced slave to community journalism, might have been a mite modest of vision.

Surely he might have considered worthy the documentation of such touchstones as divorce, DWI, and which rest home grandma got consigned to. After all, to those touched by such fates, the experience may verily impact local health and welfare, or at least resonate like virgin gossip among the chattering class.

By the mid-1980s, community journalism was the must-do topic at every editorial conference worthy of an expense-account junket; some, indeed, were useful. Focus groups, too, were the rage. Suddenly, it seemed, everybody at the large metro papers was seeking the secret of the little guys, how their coverage worked, how they added readers while the big papers were losing, or failing to gain, subscribers in outlying areas. Newspapers, so concerned with their circulation, were sending teams of senior managers from one metro paper to the next to find answers. Favorite story: A Texas metro sent a team to study how a large California paper was luring suburban readers—while, in the same week, the California paper sent a delegation to the Texas paper to study its suburban operation.

Interestingly, if one reads a summary of TPA's educational efforts over the last fifty years, it would be impossible not to be impressed with the organization's professional prescience. Long before the newsroom mantra called for crisper, better writing, tighter editing, and better use of graphics and photos—well before the lemming-like rush to outdo *USA Today*—the Texas Press Association was running workshops and seminars on such. You can check it out.

When I got out of Baylor in 1967 I had two job offers—one as a reporter at the *Baytown Sun* for $90 a week, the other as an ad salesman for the *Temple Daily Telegram* at $135 a week. I took the Baytown job. So much for a Baylor education.

I went to Baytown because I wanted to work with two young editors there, former Baylor students Henry Holcomb and Bob Rothe, and the paper, under the leadership of the Hartman family, had strong Baylor ties, which in those days seemed to mean more.

Holcomb and Rothe had already had already worked for other newspapers, and to work under them would prove invaluable over my next professional thirty-five years. Rothe was as good a news editor—and story editor—as I would ever work for. Henry was an exacting assignment editor whose reputation for uncommonly thorough and thoughtful reportage was near legendary among Baylor journalism students. Henry, who never saw an ambulance he couldn't chase, carried so many police radios in the trunk of his Pontiac sedan you'd think he was pimping for Radio Shack. His motto would have done any Boy Scout proud: Be prepared, or be embarrassed. He was a super mentor, and his lessons would stick.

A few hours after the *Columbia* explosion in February 2003, I was sitting on the side of a road near Palestine in East Texas, waiting for a *Star-Telegram* reporter to complete an interview at a nearby gas station. Suddenly a sheriff's car sped by. Without thinking, I took off, trying to catch the car, reaching nearly 100 mph. The chase led to the first piece of shuttle debris we had seen and a series of interviews with witnesses. All because of what Henry had once told me: If you ever see a cop car speed by, follow him, because you need to be there, too. It was automatic, after all these years.

There were other lessons Baytown afforded, the kind that come only with the community newspaper experience.

Late one afternoon somebody knocked at my apartment door. It was a teenage girl that lived just down the street. She had read my feature about one of her neighbors.

"But you got it all wrong, Mr. Blackman. He isn't the nice man, the hero you made him out top be. He cusses little kids and threatens to shoot our dogs if they poop in his yard."

Never again did I write a single-source personality profile.

Sometimes the small-paper education could be more subtle and complex, more nuanced.

While making my police rounds one morning I learned that someone had complained about a local madam and her working girls, who ran a vibrant enterprise out near the refinery area known as Old Baytown. I was immediately interested, probably for reasons likely more immediate than another coveted byline. Like a good reporter, I called aside one of the assistant chiefs to get more information.

"Nah," he said. "You don't want to do that story. If we have to close the place down, then the customers will just get all agitated, and the next thing you know we'll have wives getting beat up all over town. You don't want that, do you? Think of this as a public service. Just wait. Every six months or so one of our preachers will start sermonizing about the house and the girls, and we'll shut it down for a few days. Been doing this for years. I'll see you get a tip on the story."

Of such I never learned in journalism, or on big-city police beats. I never did the story, and moved on before the next sermon on the, well, house.

Finally, a belated appreciation for, and lesson from, my year in Baytown community journalism.

Our managing editor, Preston Pendergrass, a gentleman of good cheer and ability who lived dangerously when it came to transporting his false teeth, told me there might be a good story in a shoeshine man who had just died: a real nice fellow, had been a fixture on the barbershop scene forever, was nice to kids and old people, on and on.

Of course, what I was limited to was a feature obituary, which meant I had to interview anyone who knew him, which included several prominent Baytown citizens. The man's name was Tamp, and he indeed was as nice and as generous of spirit as everyone said. He spent his last dollars on food for the hungry and took care of anybody in the neighborhood who was ill. He himself was forever in great pain—he had lost his legs when he fell under a train when he was a kid.

I did the story, which I was proud of, three columns on page one, even though it was clearly overwritten, overwrought. Over the next few days I got a few calls from readers thanking me for the story, and even our publisher, Fred Hartman, came by my desk to say nice job.

Never gave it another thought. Then in May 2003, thirty-seven years later, I got a visit from Henry Holcomb, now a reporter with the *Philadelphia Inquirer*. (By the mid-1980s, we three from Baytown—Holcomb, Rothe,

Blackman—were all working as editors at the *Inquirer*). We had all stayed in touch over the years.

On the day Henry came we got to talking about our Baytown days, and eventually about the story about Tamp.

"Did you know," he said, "that was the first time a feature story about a black person ever ran in the *Baytown Sun*?"

I didn't. Didn't have a clue.

"There was a lot of rumbling in the building about the story, people worried what readers would do."

Who was worried, I still don't know. But I know that nothing ever got in the paper that ever ran counter to management's wishes. (Amazing how the backshop foreman—and printers—had a hotline to the publisher's office.) This was a time, in the '60s, when it was still common for news about minorities, if it ran at all, to be displayed deep inside most newspapers. Just the way it was.

It would be nice to say that Henry and I fought to place the story on page one out of both courage and a heightened sense of journalistic groundbreak. But we didn't. To us, we just thought it was a pretty good story the readers might enjoy, and Henry just wanted to make sure it got good play.

"I never thought about Tamp being black," he recalled recently.

Recounting that day in the newsroom, I think we both now sense an opportunity lost, like an easy merit badge being passed by. But the important thing was that the story got in with management's blessing, was read, and was talked about. Who says naiveté doesn't have its own rewards?

It was a story stumbled on, assigned to a rookie reporter with more enthusiasm than talent and eventually shepherded to a favored position by a savvy editor who insisted it be made easy for readers to find: Page One.

Simple as that. Modest barrier broken. Accidently. But broken by the most basic of newspaper imperatives: There was a good story to tell. Tamp the shine man, whom most everybody knew but few knew much about. His color never came up in *The Baytown Sun* newsroom, not while the story was being written or edited or after it was published. This being Texas 1968, top management undoubtedly took some heat from readers, but to its everlasting grace never let us know.

John Dycus says all good publishers in small towns must have focus and courage. I prefer to think that management exhibited courage that day with Tamp's story and maybe, just maybe, brought a little more understanding and tolerance among people in an era sorely bereft of both.

Surely the best, most lasting, and most rewarding legacy of community journalism to Texas and the journalistic world beyond is this: It gave fledgling reporters and editors their first professional job, trained them in the basics, whetted their curiosity for the hows and whys of life's inexplicable, instilled a steady discipline, and, in many ways, inspired them to be better than they had a right to be.

Ask any of today's most prominent journalists, and they will likely tell you how they, too, got their start on a weekly or small daily. Who hasn't, fresh out of J-school, talent considerably south of talent and dream, been admonished at interview's close by some belly-over-belt big-city managing editor: "Kid, get some experience on a little paper and come back in a year or two."

Good advice. Terrific advice. Forget that the big-city editor just wanted you to go away.

Today our community journalism thrives, rambunctious, nurturing, opinionated, recording our dreams and deeds, failings and flaws. And it does it the old-fashioned way. Reporters shoe-leather through neighborhoods taking notes, and then try to bring sense and order to the daily goings-on in their community, and all the while opening a window for future historians to understand our past.

More than 500 TPA papers—weeklies, semiweeklies, and nonmetro dailies—every day set forth to record an earnest and detailed diary of Texas life, recording to varying degrees births and deaths and graduations and even divorced drunks on the road to see Grandma in the rest home, and so much more.

Interview the mayor, police chief, or the nearest college professor, and suddenly you have an analysis or backgrounder, or if you are really lucky, a trend story. Publishers like trend stories, those with lots of names. Chances are it will be played right there on page one next to the big-haired blonde announced as FFA Queen for 2005, above the photo of the season's first bale of cotton ginned and the local congressman's weekly column, and beside the forty-seven-pound yellow cat caught on stink-baited trot line and below the smiling picture and 42-point, three-column headline heralding the coming home of the football-star-turned-marine, bemedaled galore for freedom's fight, posthumously.

Whatever, as they say, it will be, all of it, readable, relevant, and intensely personal, and may well make a difference. Further, it will be forging the continuum of community newspapering and Texas history while burnishing the Texas persona along the way. The way we were. The way we are.

MICHAEL BLACKMAN *is a former reporter and editor at the* Fort Worth Star-Telegram, *as well as an editor at papers in Ohio, New York, and Pennsylvania.*

CHAPTER 5

What Newspapers Are Supposed to Do

THE EXAMPLE OF SIX COURAGEOUS PUBLISHERS

WANDA GARNER CASH

Most newspapers strive to reflect their community—celebrating the wondrous, never-ceases-to-amaze goodness of people, but neither omitting nor glossing over their all-too-human foibles.

And even when newspapers report the sad, the nefarious, or the ugly, something good usually will result: overthrown corruption, resolution of conflict, a triumph of spirit.

Publishers' roles may change, switching from unabashed booster to objective observer, depending on the community's geography, size, and demographics. But on the whole, they are committed to the core values of newspaper journalism: balance, accuracy, community leadership, public access, editorial judgment, and credibility.

The mission to tell the story of the people and issues unique to a newspaper's geographical coordinates means reporting on tax increases and crime and governmental fraud alongside Little League scores and church activities, livestock prices and the mosquito count. The best community papers reach beyond that boundary, striving to translate and localize what else is going on in the world, helping readers become bona fide citizens of the global village and providing insight to what's happening in our own backyard.

When a newspaper uncovers something we would rather keep hidden, suddenly the illuminating scrutiny readers clamor for changes into distrust and suspicion.

The editor's job gets even lonelier as his readers question his motivation and hometown loyalty.

In *Travels with Charley*, John Steinbeck touched on this phenomenon, describing his time as a newspaper reporter: "When people are engaged in something they are not proud of, they do not welcome witnesses. In fact, they come to believe the witness causes the trouble."

Readers often are vexed when editors and publishers report bad news, when they take an unpopular stand on an issue.

Small-town editors can't hide in the anonymity that cloaks their metro brethren. Awkward encounters are inevitable in a town where they shop, pray, and volunteer alongside the subjects on their news pages.

And in spite of wags who say editors and reporters seek out or exploit sensational stories just to sell papers, I don't know of any legitimate news-paperman or newspaperwoman who takes that approach. Many publishers lament the isolation that comes with the job. They regret the friendship-ending coverage that just can't be spiked, but they continue to write the editorial, publish the story.

It's not courage, they say, it's just doing the job. Doing what newspapers are supposed to do.

In the following columns and editorials, editors and publishers describe the importance of that job and the personal challenges that make it hard.

WANDA GARNER CASH *is editor and publisher of the* Baytown Sun. *A community newspaper veteran with more than twenty-five years' experience, Cash previously served as executive editor of the* Brazosport Facts, *assistant managing editor of the* Galveston County Daily News, *and editor of the* Kerrville Daily Times. *Before moving into daily newspaper work, Cash was the owner, editor, and publisher of the* Ingram News, *a 2,000-circulation weekly in the Texas Hill Country. She was the 125th president of the Texas Press Association.*

In 1962, the *Pecos Independent and Enterprise* uncovered the fertilizer fraud story that brought West Texas to national attention and sent Billie Sol Estes to prison for defrauding the federal government. Newspaper editor Oscar Griffin Jr. coordinated the coverage and wrote the stories and editorials that won the Pulitzer Prize for Local Reporting in 1963.

AN OUTRAGE TO INTEGRITY

Oscar Griffin Jr., *Pecos Independent and Enterprise*, May 31, 1962

If suits filed, both criminal and civil, in the Estes fiasco are even partially correct—and we certainly have little reason to doubt they are—why is the government considering doing business with the receiver of this mess?

It appears, from evidence presented in the courts of inquiry and other investigations, that the entire plan of attack upon the accepted principles of business ethics and morals progressed in the following manner: The empire builder attacked the anhydrous ammonia industry by selling the fertilizer

Billy Sol Estes, 1962. *From Shel Hershorn Photograph Collection, Center for American History, The University of Texas at Austin. DI Number 01424.*

ridiculously below the wholesale cost. However, being unable to maintain the losses involved in running all large and small business out of the market, a plan was devised whereby losses would be negated by the sale of non-existent ammonia tanks and a long-term plan of repayment of mortgages devised.

As evidence thus far presented has confirmed, many honest and hardworking fertilizer dealers were forced out of business. Thusly, illegal money in the hands of a ruthless competitor was responsible for the complete ruin of many people.

This same picture is presented in the grain, newspaper, funeral parlor and many other local businesses—an unlimited supply of illegal money forcing those who have invested honestly obtained capital to compete in an unfair market.

Viewing the premise that all the businesses now in the hands of Mr. Harry Moore were acquired with "tainted money," where does the United States government's motivation for doing business with the receivership morally or legally fit into the picture?

Do the taxpayers of this nation have any obligation whatsoever to pay the debts of or meet obligations of such an illegitimate monstrosity which caused undue hardships on so many legal business institutions?

If the truth were known, the millions now owed by the Estes receivership would in all probability be matched in losses by honest businessmen who struggled to compete with this enterprise.

If the present administration, or any past or future administration, feels obligated to pay debts arising from such an operation, by storing grain in its facilities, when there are ample other facilities available, it must recognize a political potential or a moral obligation which we fail to honor.

We, and many others, have worked hard and under very trying conditions exposing this outrage to the integrity of the American people.

We have not been blinded by dollars in the past and we will not be blinded by dollars in the future. The businessmen of Texas have no obligation to pay debts created by the Estes fiasco—neither does the American taxpayer.

OSCAR GRIFFIN JR. *was also editor of the* Canyon News. *He worked for the* Houston Chronicle *from 1962 to 1969 as a reporter and White House correspondent. From 1969 to 1974, Griffin served as assistant director of public affairs for the U.S. Department of Transportation. After his work in Washington he returned to Texas and founded Griffin Well Service, an oil company in El Campo. Also in that time he graduated from the Harvard School of Business.*

Griffin received a bachelor of arts degree in journalism from the University of Texas at Austin in 1958.

Source: *Who's Who in America*, 52nd, 51st, 50th 49th, 48th editions; *Who's Who in the South and Southwest*, 24th edition.

On June 7, 1998, a black man, James Byrd Jr. was beaten and dragged to death by three white men in a pickup truck on a quiet country road near Jasper, Texas. Those three men were arrested on June 8, and subsequently tried and sentenced for their horrific act, which was found to be a racially motivated hate murder. William "Bill" King and Russell Brewer were sentenced to death, and Shawn Berry was sentenced to life in prison. The following columns by the *Jasper Newsboy* managing editor and its publisher reflect on how the murder touched their community.

FIVE YEARS LATER, THERE IS MORE

Julie Webb, *Jasper Newsboy*, June 4, 2003

Just as there are defining moments in the lives of individuals, there are defining moments in the life of a community. One of Jasper's defining moments came five years ago.

Five. Five is the number on everyone's mind this week. The fifth anniversary, five years since . . . Where are the principals five years later?

This Saturday, June 7, 2003, it will have been five years since James Byrd Jr. was sadistically murdered in what became the most notorious hate crime of the 20th century.

And yes, it happened in Jasper, Texas. And yes, the community circled Byrd's family in a feeble attempt to shelter them from the horror, and in a larger sense to protect ourselves.

And yes, the eyes of the world turned to Jasper and asked: How did you allow this to happen? What kind of people are you? And some, like a London newspaper, bore headlines such as, "The Town That Shamed America."

And yes, it hurt.

This week, newspapers across the country are recapping the saga of Jasper. Showtime will premier the made-for-TV movie *Jasper, Texas* and *People* magazine will feature Jasper County Sheriff Billy Rowles and the role he played in bringing Byrd's killers to justice.

For most people in America, the story is informative and frightening and, at least for a brief time, it allows them to believe, "See we're not so bad. That didn't, couldn't happen here."

But, for the town of Jasper it isn't just a story. It is a cross to bear, onward and upward, with perhaps the opportunity to grow and strengthen and then and only then, enlighten others.

Five years later.

Personally, I can't address the Byrd family. That they have endured the unendurable with a grace I have yet to understand is beyond explanation by lesser beings such as me.

Time and again, I have addressed the community, stressing education as a vehicle for change and compassion as the emotion to allow us to survive the dark days and move forward toward the light.

And yet, the world beyond Jasper is asking again, "Have you changed? Where are you now?"

I don't want to answer. Partially, because the answer evolves daily and is difficult to put into words. Partially, because only those who intimately lived the last five years of Jasper could possibly begin to understand.

But, mostly I shrink from answering because it's exhausting. It's the elephant in the room I would like to ignore.

Five years ago, three white men beat and tortured and dragged a black man to death in Jasper, Texas. The community did its best to unite, and continues the best way it knows how to fight discrimination and hatred. Sometimes it is successful and sometimes it is not.

It was a defining moment. But, it was not the defining moment. There is more to this community.

There are schools and businesses and local governments. There are sports and bands and choirs. There are churches and family reunions and celebrations. There is more, more than what happened here five years ago. There are more defining moments ahead for Jasper.

More is what I want to think about and write about and be part of. And that's my answer to all those who question.

Five years later, there is more.

JULIE WEBB *is contributing editor at the* Jasper Newsboy. *She began her journalism career in 1966 with a teen column for the* Baytown Sun. *At $1 a column inch, it was, she said, her most lucrative writing job to date. Webb also served as ad salesperson and business manager for the* Lockhart Post-Register *and general manager for the* Fredericksburg Radio-Post.

In the fall of 1999, she covered the third capital murder trial in the death of James Byrd Jr. for the Jasper Newsboy, *and joined the paper full-time in January 2000. She was the first journalist on the scene and the only one present in Sabine County during the first crucial hours after the space shuttle* Columbia *tragedy in 2003. In 2002 she won a first place award for investigative reporting from the National Newspaper Association.*

IS THERE AN INVISIBLE WALL THAT KEEPS SOME FROM ACHIEVING?

Willis Webb, *Jasper Newsboy*, September 2, 1998

"You can't hold a man down without staying down with him."
Booker T. Washington

If you feel you're being watched closely from two directions, you're probably right.

The world is viewing us from "above" through a microscope. A group of people in town is scrutinizing the leadership and thus, the community from the inside. What perception viewers derive in each case is extremely significant and will shape what people think of Jasper for many years to come.

The internal examination will dictate the shape of this town much more than the external one, although world attention certainly shouldn't be ignored. It's just that the internal one, if not answered, could turn Jasper even more topsy-turvy.

When I discussed coming to Jasper to edit and publish this newspaper just over seven years ago, one of many concerns was race relations. I asked and was told they were excellent. And, on the surface at least, that was and is true.

My question didn't mean that I feared race riots or anything of that nature. I came here from an area where my neighborhood would have almost passed for the United Nations in its ethnic make-up. The entire area was rich in its diversity. Being someone who has been accused of being a mix of idealism and optimism with just a dash of cynicism, I suppose I expected "excellent" to mean that Jasper was like my east Fort Bend County neighborhood with an East Texas flavor.

Overall I am quite happy and pleased with Jasper.

Julie and I decided some time ago that this would be our home through retirement and our later years—God willing. We love Jasper and the people here, all of you.

However, if we're all honest with ourselves, and each other, "excellent" does describe just the surface of race relations here. There are troubles that rumble just beneath the surface, but they are not troubles that can't be solved.

Walter Diggles hit on at least part of it in a conversation he and I had several years ago when I put the question of race relations to him. He said, "I don't feel there is very much discrimination with regard to race here. Most discrimination here, and many other places, is economic."

That statement, I believe, is endemic to that which is almost roiling just beneath the surface here.

As to the surface relations, there is a segment of African American society here that has gained a measure of economic and political success. With that has come acceptance in the larger society, dominated for years by Caucasian Americans. The economically and politically successful Caucasian Americans and African Americans interact in society, business and politics.

While some people will tell you, honestly, that pursing a good education and hard work have afforded them the economic, social and political gains and freedoms, there is a system in place (and to which no one can or will lay claim) that limits accessibility to that surface group of either color. As one man put it, "they let you reach out to a certain point, then there's the wall."

We are kidding ourselves if we think America is classless or ever will be until that time of the perfect afterlife which the faith of so many promises.

I'm afraid that economic discrimination of which Walter Diggles spoke will be kept alive to some degree by human nature. But, it is possible to see that everyone has the best possible chance for a fine education and for economic opportunity.

There are young people in this town who have started out with stars in their eyes, believing they were going to grab that golden ring on the carousel of life. They may have begun on a simple promise such as taking easy classes to stay eligible in athletics. Then they saw those hopes dashed against that invisible wall which, at that point, consisted of not enough education to go with the athletic prowess that was supposed to take them to higher education and all the things it could attain.

We can't fulfill everyone's dream to the point of being in the wealthiest class, or the most "socially acceptable class" or the "political leader class," but we can educate everyone so they can attain the highest level of success possible. And, we can see that there aren't any barriers to someone's natural ability and their willingness to work hard enough to have all the necessary things in life regardless of race or economic beginnings.

Then we will have satisfied the eyes of the rest of the world looking down through the microscope at Jasper. But, most importantly, we will have brought those other eyes from just beneath the surface to the top.

OBJECTIVE JOURNALISM MUST PREVAIL OVER EMOTIONAL TIES

Willis Webb, *Jasper Newsboy*, November 10, 1999

There has been so much about our Jasper news situation that has occupied my mind lately. Here we are in the midst of the supposed final trial of the Byrd murder trilogy. So much is happening in this trial that one's mind can almost suffer from information overload with just a single day's events. And, that doesn't count emotional involvement.

What really made some things crystallize in my mind was in the courtroom Monday afternoon. In walked Betty Byrd Boatner and her father, James Byrd Sr., to observe the hearing for a requested change of venue for Shawn Berry, the third man accused of killing James Byrd Jr.

Prior to last year's horrendous crime, I didn't know any member of the Byrd family, nor anyone (that I knew of) connected with any of the defendants.

I was quickly introduced to the Byrd family and thus began an involvement of respect and great admiration for those members I have come to know. My first introduction was happenstance, on Tuesday morning after the Sunday murder, when Clara Byrd Taylor came to the office early, looking for a copy of the *Beaumont Enterprise*, which contained the first press report of her brother's death.

There was no one else available at that hour to help her find what she needed, so I did.

In only a couple of minutes' time, I was so impressed with her dignity and grace under what had to be the most difficult of circumstances. You could sense and almost feel the great inner strength that every member of this remarkable family exudes.

In short order I met Betty in the matter of another news event, the announcement of her daughter's engagement and approaching marriage. An engagement party on that fateful night had been the last time family members had seen "Son" Byrd.

The rest of life, such as the significant event of betrothal, went on.

Mike Journee and I went to the Byrd home that week and talked to Clara,

Papa Byrd, and Mama Stella. While Mike and I were inhibited in conducting an interview by the great sympathy we felt for a Jasper family in such a monumental tragedy, we were at the same time overwhelmed by their grace, dignity and inner strength.

Then, on that Friday, June 12, I decided as a Jasperite (not as a newsman) to attend the wake service at Greater New Bethel Baptist Church. To my shock and surprise, I was called on by Brother Kenneth Lyons to say a few words. I managed to mutter something about going to the Byrd home and feeling inadequate at having nothing in the way of real comfort to offer the family but that James Byrd Sr. and his remarkable family had offered me one of the greatest lessons of faith in God that I have ever witnessed.

As I left the lectern to return to my seat, Papa Byrd reached and took my hand and shook it. I was overwhelmed and almost overcome.

Over the past 17 months I have had a number of occasions to see and visit with the Byrd family.

Not too many months ago, I went to the Byrd home on another occasion to see and photograph a quilt made by a group of women from across the nation commemorating "Son" Byrd's life. In the course of the visit I saw Betty Boatner again, and held and played with her granddaughter.

Monday in the courtroom, Betty and I recalled that visit as she, her father, and I visited.

As I thought about that visit and looked about the courtroom, I thought about being a small-town journalist and about how well most of us in community newspapers know the people we write about. I pondered my own involvement with so many other than the Byrd family in this case.

Naturally I know Judge Joe Bob Golden, District Attorney Guy James Gray and his staff, as well as Sheriff Billy Rowles and his folks.

In addition I have come to know some people or have resurrected contacts and relationships with others who have become news figures in this case.

There is Bobby Lively, a former Jasper High football great who has fought some tremendous odds to stay on track for a college education. Lively drives home from Henderson State in Arkansas to stand by his friend Shawn Berry and maintains he just can't believe he was involved in the killing.

There was Berry's two-year-old son, Montana, playing at the county jail with several small African American children. He was hugging each child and displaying the loving innocence we all pray could engulf the world.

Defense attorney Lum Hawthorn, cast in a position not made for universal popularity, comes across as a caring individual and a gentleman.

The Byrd case has put me in touch on several occasions with an old acquaintance who played a role in my start in journalism: Dan Rather, who chaired a college scholarship committee that gave a then-high school senior a financial boost with the award.

Oddly enough, an old acquaintance plays yet another role in these proceedings. Charles L. "Chip" Babcock, attorney for CBS producer Mary Mapes on a press freedom issue, represented me 10 years ago in fighting for my right to work in my chosen profession. Chip took my case (well into the proceedings) because he was "appalled" by what he felt was being done to me. After an almost two-year battle, we prevailed.

So it is with small-town journalism. I have a tremendous amount of information about the characters and roles in this constantly unfolding drama. I also have some emotional investment in many of them.

Yet, I find, because of years of training and because of all journalists' commitment to the straight reporting of the news, I am able to do my job, to look at each development in its context of news and to report it and how it reflects on Jasper to our readers.

In my examination of this situation, it was natural to always fall back on journalism training, but I also concluded that small-town involvement and experience also teaches most of us who live in them, to not just cherish relationships but to be able to rise above the fray when necessary and make judgments that will be fair to our town and its residents. I think that latter measurement can be applied to small-town juries, too.

It will be interesting to see how we stand up to the test.

WILLIS WEBB *has more than 50 years' experience as a journalist and community newspaper editor-publisher, receiving the Texas Press Association "Golden 50" award in 2002. Since May 20, 1991, he has been editor and publisher of the* Jasper Newsboy. *In 1997 he was the first weekly newspaper person to receive the Hearst Corporation's Eagle Award for outstanding individual accomplishment in journalism.*

He previously published and edited newspapers in Teague, Galena Park, Rosenberg, Cleveland, Conroe, Lockhart, Fredericksburg, and Missouri City.

Webb was the 124th president of the Texas Press Association and is currently chairman of its board.

In the fall of 1995, a group of Baptist ministers called for a boycott of the *Galveston County Daily News*, alleging racial bias and discrimination. At issue was the paper's coverage of an investigation into illegal spending of city funds and mismanagement of funds at the Galveston Municipal Court.

The boycott was in reaction to an editorial by publisher Dolph Tillotson, who called on the city council to remove City Manager Doug Matthews.

The Baptist ministers association, a predominantly African American group, organized the boycott and a rally in support of Matthews, who is black.

In response to the call for the subscription and advertising boycott, Tillotson said the paper's coverage of the millions of dollars unaccounted for at city hall was tough and aggressive, but fair. "We simply have tried to cover city government and take a stand on the opinion page that was important to all citizens, black and white."

The city council fired the city manager in December 1995. The action drew the ire of Matthews's attorney, state representative Ron Wilson, D-Houston, who described the council's firing of Matthews as a "low-tech lynching."

Throughout the coverage and attendant controversy, Tillotson encouraged the community to focus the debate on fiscal issues rather than race. The following editorial and column are examples of his direct approach to readers.

DOING JUST AS A NEWSPAPER SHOULD

Dolph Tillotson, *Galveston County Daily News*, November 16, 1995

Some readers called upon other readers yesterday to boycott this newspaper. They object to our coverage of the ongoing controversy surrounding Galveston City Manager Doug Matthews.

No business relishes the idea of a boycott. Nobody likes being criticized. However, the *Daily News* has done its job as a good newspaper should. We will continue in that effort.

Our job is to seek out and cover news that affects the lives of our readers. We report news objectively and then take stands on those issues that have the greatest impact on the community. We do this not to dictate opinions to our readers but to help them make informed decisions.

The issues here are not black and white, but green. They are financial. The *Daily News* has been monitoring and reporting on the handling of public funds because it dramatically affects the lives of our readers.

The dollar amounts, which appear to have been lost through mismanagement, total more than $10 million by most estimates. To put that in perspective, that's about: one-fourth of Galveston's annual operating budget; one-half of the total amount Galveston collects annually in property taxes; enough to replace the sand on Galveston's beaches—twice; enough to put 100 or more additional police officers on the streets for three years.

Our coverage of Matthews's conduct in office has been tough and aggressive, but it's been fair. We have applied the same standard in covering his office that we apply to all public officials.

Our strong, clear stands on the Opinion page have been written to educate and inform—not preach. We have always encouraged and included opposing positions. Our stands have been tempered by giving Matthews and his supporters virtually unlimited access to the same space to state his case over and over again.

We may have been more outspoken than some newspapers, but Galveston is a community that values plain talk, and we don't pull punches.

Our coverage never has dealt in personal attacks. It has focused on issues of broad and fundamental public importance. We believe these are issues a good newspaper simply has to cover. Most of our readers expect no less of us.

In the future, we will continue to do our job. We are, in fact, proud of the work of the newspaper's staff, which has fought hard against stiff resistance to tell the story to our readers completely and fairly. The effort has taken courage and many, many hours of hard work. Because of it, the people of Galveston have a much clearer picture of how their city government works. That is what newspapers are supposed to do.

THREATS ROUTINE, AND ROUTINELY FAIL

Dolph Tillotson, *Galveston County Daily News*, December 10, 1995

In these days of controversy and criticism of the newspaper, friends have taken to offering me sympathy. I appreciate the thought, but the truth is I wouldn't change places with anybody.

For the most part, the work I do is just plain fun. Being at the newspaper puts you in the middle of a community's triumphs, tragedies and controversies. For most of us, there's no place we'd rather be.

It amazes me to talk with friends who don't like the work they do.

I get up every morning eager to see the product we produced last night. When I walk through the office door in the morning, the aroma of ink and newsprint lifts my spirits.

Being a newspaper editor has at least a couple of downsides. They, too, are a part of my profession's rough charm.

For me, maybe the worst is that the paper never is perfect. It's a big product produced in a hurry by people with too much to do.

Another downside is that someone is trying all the time to threaten us. That is because we are the bridge to you. There are many people who want to control what you read. Sometimes they threaten lawsuits (a couple of times a week). Sometimes they threaten boycotts. Sometimes they threaten to punch your nose. It's all the same thing, and it's a routine part of my job.

In the time I have lived in Galveston, people have threatened lawsuits more times than I can count. Often that comes from somebody whose son or husband got arrested, and they want to keep it out of the paper.

The last people to picket our building were supporters of a gambling referendum. The time before that, it was the Ku Klux Klan. We refused a hateful advertisement the Klan wanted in the paper.

There have been two boycotts in my eight years, one by the longshoreman's union and now by some supporters of suspended Galveston City Manager Doug Matthews.

I don't know much, but I do know this: A newspaper that lets people push it around with threats isn't much of a newspaper.

My basic approach is this: I'll talk to almost anybody about almost anything anytime. We are wrong sometimes, and I listen to questions and complaints virtually every day. In other words, thoughtful persuasion often works to influence our opinions and what we publish.

What I will not do is give in to a threat, ever. If I did, the Ku Klux Klan would run your newspaper one day. The unions would run it the next. The Democrats and Republicans could run it on alternate weeks. If the Libertarians got organized, they could run it, too, just by making a threat.

The result would be that no one could believe anything they read in these pages. I can't and won't let that happen.

DOLPH TILLOTSON *is president and publisher of Galveston Newspapers Inc. and a vice president of Southern Newspapers Inc. He is a former chairman of the Legislative Advisory Committee for Texas Press Association/Texas Daily Newspaper Association. He also is a former president of TDNA and the winner of its Pat Taggart Award.*

Tillotson's first newspaper job was as a stringer for the Tuscaloosa (Ala.) News *at eighteen. From 1973 to 1975 he was general manager of the* Natchez (Miss.) Democrat. *From 1975 to 1980 he was publisher of the* Oskaloosa (Iowa) Herald. *From 1980 to 1981, Tillotson moved back to Tuscaloosa and became president of Boone Newspapers Inc. In 1981 he moved to Natchez, retained the job of president of BNI, and became publisher of the* Democrat, *where he remained until 1987, when he came to Galveston.*

In January 1996, the *Brazosport Facts* reported on local and state officials who went goose hunting on a private island in Canada. What made the story newsworthy was who the hunters were and who paid for the trip.

The two-day hunting party included a state senator, a county judge, a city councilman, and a school superintendent. Hosting the outing at his company's lodge was the plant manager for one of Brazoria County's largest industries. The trip took place about a week after county commissioners approved tax abatements for the company.

The officials said it was a pleasure trip and that no business was discussed. The company said there was no intent to reward anyone. "It was all done as a friendship sort of thing. I didn't view it as a lobbying effort," the senator told the newspaper.

Braced for the inevitable reaction, *Facts* publisher Bill Cornwell faced the challenge of reporting on hometown controversy and ran the stories. In his Sunday column, Cornwell talked about his values as a newsman and his personal striving for fairness.

THE PUBLIC HAD A RIGHT TO KNOW

Bill Cornwell, *Brazosport Facts*, February 4, 1996

A tough thing happened this past week. We ran a story that involved my friends.

Was it factual? Yes, I think it was. Did the general public have a right to know? I believe they did. Were they involved in something illegal? Probably not, but there are those in authority who have yet to rule. Will it change things for the better? It might.

Hit me with your best shot. I don't think there is a question that I haven't asked myself.

I was faced with a situation most journalists dread. People you love and respect become names in a story.

Few people understand the media. I have trouble at times understanding the media and I'm in the media business.

What makes a story? Why is one news story more important than another? Why do negative stories rise in importance over positive events? What is the motivation behind a report? Who are they (the media) out to get? Do they really print the sensational stuff just to sell papers?

The process of gathering and prioritizing news is difficult to explain. Sometimes it is equally as difficult to justify.

Just like the lawyers and politicians we love to hate, journalists rank no higher in public opinion and yet our basic freedoms depend on the health of all three. Isn't it strange how we view those we have to trust? But, I truly understand the sentiment.

I got into this business because I wanted to make a difference. I worked to become a publisher because I wanted to ensure that the news was printed impartially without prejudice toward race, creed, financial status or social position.

That's all very noble until you get right down to it.

This isn't the first time I've had to publish a story about someone close to me. But, it is the first time I've felt like writing about it.

There are those who cheered when we printed the news about a local industry's questionable hunting trip to Canada this past week. Many others didn't agree it was even news at all.

I considered the information and obviously felt it was worth public consumption. Being the newspaper of record for Brazoria County, it is our job to report the facts and dispel rumors.

The sad thing about the story is that industries and business in Brazoria County have long been entertaining clients and politicians. I believe there have been abuses and I think some "good old boy" politicians have taken full advantage of the process.

If any good at all came out of last week's story, it is that at least maybe now the "good old boys" will think twice before they play loose with the power of their office. If they don't heed this lesson, it's obvious we won't hesitate to write about them.

To me the Canadian trip was a simple matter of bad judgment. Someone should have been more aware of how it might appear. But, knowing the people involved, I really think it was just a bunch of friends trying to get together to enjoy each others company.

If that is so, then why did I let the story stand?

I asked myself the standard question, "If I didn't personally know the players involved, would I still allow the story to be printed?" The answer was yes.

It doesn't matter what I think personally. It doesn't matter whether I know them as friends. A trip was taken, bad judgment was used and the public had a right to know.

BILL CORNWELL *graduated from the University of Texas with a journalism degree in 1978. He began his career with Southern Newspapers Inc. at the* Baytown Sun.

In 1987 he became the editor and publisher of the Daily Sentinel, *an SNI paper in Scottsboro, Alabama. After five years in Alabama, Cornwell returned to his native state in 1992 to become editor and publisher of the* Brazosport Facts *in Clute, Texas. He is a former president of the Texas Daily Newspaper Association, the 2003 winner of its Frank Mayborn Award for Community Leadership, and a member of the Texas Press Association and the TPA/TDNA Legislative Advisory Council.*

The following three editorials were written by Ben R. Ezzell, editor and publisher of the *Canadian Record.* They were published at the midpoint of this country's engagement in the Vietnam War, a war that at its peak involved half a million American servicemen and women and that during its history claimed over 58,000 American lives.

In the Texas Panhandle, those who spoke in opposition to the war were immediately branded as Communists and traitors. The risk of doing so, both personal and financial, was great.

For Ezzell's outspoken opposition to the war, he and his family became the target of violent threats, and the Canadian Record became the target of a well-organized boycott. A boycott that was not long lasting, but one that made clear the perils awaiting those who not only defend the freedoms of speech and of the press, but also observe them in their daily lives.

Ben Ezzell, editor of the *Canadian Record*.
Courtesy the Texas Press Association.

Following Ezzell's sudden death after heart surgery in January 1993, Lieutenant Governor Bob Bullock, who was a personal friend and admirer of Ezzell's, made this statement:

Ben Ezzell was the conscience of newspapering in Texas. Truth and common sense were his creed in all things big and small. He was absolutely fearless when it came to standing up for individual and human rights. Neither the threats of fire bombs nor the siren of personal ego changed Ben Ezzell's course or convictions, not in business, not in politics and not in friendships. Texas has lost a great man, and I have lost a good personal friend of many years standing. I hope that Nan and family find some solace in knowing that their grief is shared by many.

AMERICAN TRAGEDY

Ben R. Ezzell, *Canadian Record*, May 16, 1970

The My Lai massacre last year was a long way off, and the victims were Vietnamese peasants. The Kent State massacre on Monday was in Ohio, U.S.A., and the victims were young Americans. The killers, in both instances, wore the uniforms of United States Armed Forces.

Does the great American "silent majority" still see no cause for alarm?

The televised spectacle of a wave of American soldiers in full battle array, gas masks in place, rifles at the ready, advancing on an American college campus against a rally of American college students who were gathered to protest the Vietnam war, was terrifying. When these American soldiers began firing into the unarmed ranks of collegians, first with gas grenades and later with live bullets from semi-automatic rifles, it became horrifying.

Four young American boys and girls lay dead, and others were gravely wounded. And something in the heart of our America has been desperately wounded, too.

These killers at Kent State were American soldiers, carrying weapons issued by the United States Army, firing ammunition from United States arsenals, commanded by officers commissioned by the United States Congress, and wearing uniforms of the United States Armed forces . . . uniforms which many of us have worn with pride and with honor, and now must view with shame.

President Nixon's pious statement from the White House after the massacre that "violence breeds tragedy" compounds our despair.

It does indeed, Mr. Nixon. The students at Kent State University were protesting violence which concerns them rather keenly . . . the violence of war in Vietnam . . . and in Cambodia . . . and in Laos . . . and where next, Mr. Nixon, where next?

So we meet their protest with violence, and breed more violence. The students at Kent State University on Monday fought back with the only weapons they apparently had at hand . . . sticks and stones and the tear gas canisters which had been fired at them. But who can blame these young American men and women . . . those who survived the massacre . . . if they return to the fray next time with more lethal arms?

Violence does indeed breed tragedy, Mr. Nixon . . . and more violence. American young people all over this land have been protesting violence . . . the violence of a war in Southeast Asia in which they do not believe, but in which they are being required to fight and die, to kill or be killed. And instead of hearing and heeding their protests, our national policy seems to be to meet them with displays of violent force at home, while steadily expanding the violence abroad which they, and we, deplore.

Where are we taking our tortured land? What are we doing to ourselves and our youth in this America we love?

We who are sick at heart must raise our voices in protest to our elected leaders who are sick of soul. Perhaps sooner or later, we, too, will have to be cut down by American military firing squads. This is the risk our young people are taking today to protest this expanding war. We who love America and feel responsibility for it should do no less. It is our country . . . let's save it if we can.

CREDIBILITY GAP WIDENING

Ben R. Ezzell, *Canadian Record*, May 16, 1970

If a "credibility gap" existed between the American people and the Johnson Administration, what name shall we give to the rift in credibility which is being created by the Nixon Administration in the area of foreign affairs?

It seems only yesterday . . . and it was only a handful of yesterdays ago . . . that President Nixon was assuring a nationwide television audience that no Americans had been committed to battle in Cambodia and Laos and none would be.

It was only a few months ago that President Nixon was assuring these same American citizens that American troops would be disengaged as rapidly as feasible from the conflict in South Vietnam, and there would be no expansion of the war in Southeast Asia.

Mr. Nixon has been branded a liar on both counts.

Immediately after the recent Presidential disclaimer of American casualties in Laos and Cambodia came swift evidence that American soldiers had already died in combat there, and that others were even then engaged in combat there.

And now, in an apparent reversal of policy . . . or perhaps in furtherance of what has been policy all along . . . the Commander in Chief has revealed to the nation and to a protesting and apparently impotent Congress that he has ordered a full-scale invasion of Cambodia by American troops . . . a move which can only be interpreted as expansion of the war in Southeast Asia.

Or perhaps this is merely Mr. Nixon's way of carrying out his pledge to withdraw American combat troops from South Vietnam . . . by shifting them instead into neighboring countries of the Indo-China complex.

Any way we look at it, the credibility gap is widening to frightening proportions.

SILENCE IS SODDEN

Ben R. Ezzell, *Canadian Record*, May 16, 1970

President Nixon's press chief, Herb Klein, has joined Vice-President Agnew in blasting the news media. Mr. Klein's complaint is that the media is "under-reporting" the silent majority.

Herb Klein, who is an old news-hand himself, ought to know better. People make news by doing things and saying things. The "silent majority," whoever or whatever that is, is a faceless entity which says nothing out loud and, by its own definition, does nothing unless it is done anonymously.

When it ceases to be silent and ceases to hide behind its massive anonymity, this group will certainly be heard and recognized by the news media, but until it steps out into the open, it is likely to remain unseen, unheard and unrecognized by press, radio or TV.

BEN R. EZZELL *was born May 22, 1916, in Alvord, Texas. He began his journalism career while in high school in Quitaque, and after graduating from West Texas State College in Canyon he worked on the* Claude News, *the* Floyd County Hesperian, *and the* Seminole Daily Producer. *He joined the Air Force in 1941 and served as an Air Force intelligence officer in New Guinea, the Dutch East Indies, and the Philippines. After the war, he returned to the Texas Panhandle and was managing editor of the* Hereford Brand *for two years before moving to the* Canadian. *He and his wife, Nancy, became coeditors and copublishers of the* Canadian Record *in 1948. He was a longtime member of the Panhandle Press Association and a past president of the organization. In 1992, the PPA inducted him into its Hall of Fame. He was named Canadian Man of the Year in 1968.*

CHAPTER 6

The Kingdom of West Texas

PHIL RECORD

Early in the twentieth century, many undoubtedly saw little promise in the vast, often barren, stretches of West Texas. Not Amon G. Carter Sr. He saw it as the Promised Land.

Author Jerry Flemmons stated it well in his 1978 biography of Carter, *Amon*:

> Politicians ignored West Texas. Industry spurned it. Those who went there, for business or visiting, got out as soon as they could. There was little middle class population. West Texans, poor and isolated and largely ignorant, hungered for attention. Amon Carter merely stepped in, assumed the mortgage on West Texas' future, and became its paladin, carrying the tattered banner to all America. *West Texas is important. Amon Carter said so. See! It's right here on the front page of the* Star-Telegram.[1]

And so West Texas became the *Fort Worth Star-Telegram*'s kingdom.

Carter was a product of this land, having been born in Crafton and reared in Bowie, both northwest of Fort Worth. He could not build the kingdom by himself. He gathered around him a team that was known for its vision and a willingness to put in seven-day weeks to accomplish the awesome task confronting them.

There was James M. North, the editor, who for all practical purposes guided the operations of the entire newspaper on a day-to-day basis. James R. Record was the soft-spoken managing editor who guided the news coverage. Al Shuman saw to it that the newspaper was filled with ads, and Harold Hough was in charge of the complicated process of delivering the *Star-Telegram* on time to far reaches of West Texas and western New Mexico. Bert N. Honea had the difficult task of handling the financial affairs of the newspaper, which included trying to harness Carter's freewheeling spending habits.

Amon Carter, publisher of the *Fort Worth Star-Telegram*.
*Studio portrait of Amon Carter, Amon G. Carter papers,
Special Collections, Mary Couts Burnett Library, Texas
Christian University.*

Carter was the proud and colorful peacock of the group. He loved being pictured on the front page of his newspaper greeting the famous that dropped in for a visit. He was never hesitant to shout the praise of Fort Worth and West Texas, whether greeting a distinguished visitor at home or standing on a chair in the elegant dining room of a Washington, D.C., hotel.[2]

He delighted in donning western wear, a ten-gallon hat on his head, a big cigar in his mouth, and pearl-handled six-shooters on his hips.

While Carter was constantly in the view of the public, the other five members of the *Star-Telegram* team were virtually invisible. They were content to let Amon bask in the limelight alone.

North was never comfortable with Carter's publicity-seeking ways. He went so far as to virtually ban the appearance of any member of the North and Record families in the columns of the newspaper. Family members accepted the fact that they either had to be "wed or dead" to make the *Star-Telegram*.

By today's standards, the *Star-Telegram* would not be deemed a great newspaper when it reigned over West Texas. But it did it its job well, as Flemmons noted in *Amon*:

> In all important ways, the *Star-Telegram* honored its First Amendment franchise with complete and encompassing service to its readers. That made it a good newspaper. What made it exceptional was that it served fully and faithfully an area larger than the whole of New England, did it for so long, and for much of the time without coercion of adequate competition.

Dr. DeWitt Reddick, a respected scholar and former head of the University of Texas School of Communication, said,

> The *Star-Telegram* was the best illustration of a newspaper so interwoven with the birth and growth of the country around it that people accepted it as part of their lives. It was a family member. What it did was serve. I don't believe any newspaper, anywhere, at any time, ever gave so much to its area.

I had the privilege of watching the growth, and the demise, of this newspaper kingdom from several viewpoints. I was attached to the *Star-Telegram* by blood. James Record, who served as managing editor for thirty-one years, was my father's brother. James M. North, who was editor of the newspaper from 1923 until his death in 1957, married Record's sister, Lottie.

I grew up listening to "newspaper talk."

Mr. North and Mr. Record were viewed as a team. If they ever disagreed, it was done in private. In spite of objections by their wives, the brothers-in-law inevitably turned to their favorite subject, the newspaper, at family gatherings.

"Jim, I thought we should have given that West Texas Chamber meeting in Abilene better play yesterday," I can hear Mr. North saying.

"You're right," Record would reply. "I'll talk to Presley about it tomorrow. I bet he can come up with some kind of follow-up."

He was referring to crusty state editor Presley Bryant, who had the arduous task of trying to keep up with the newspaper's hundreds of correspondents.

North had a son, Phillip Record North, who later would become associate editor of the newspaper. James Record had no children. But he wanted a Record to be a part of the paper after he was gone. So it was that he persuaded me, and later my brother, Tony, to go to work at the newspaper as copyboys.

I reported to work on July 3, 1944. From that day on, Uncle Jimmy became Mr. North and Uncle Jim became Mr. Record. That is the way I still refer to them.

When I was ready to call it a day on that July 3, I informed Mr. Record I would see him on the 5th, since I planned to be celebrating the Fourth of July the next day. He was quick to inform me that newspapermen did not get off on holidays. But I came to love the place. I loved the excitement of the news generated by World War II. I loved the smell of the place, generated by newsprint and ink. One day when someone asked me what I was going to be, I replied, "I guess a newspaperman."

I had been seduced.

When I graduated from Notre Dame in 1950, Mr. North and Mr. Record decided I should find a job in West Texas to get a feeling for this land that was so important to the newspaper. Charles Guy, editor of the *Lubbock Avalanche-Journal*, was kind enough to hire me as a reporter.

In that job I came to have a special appreciation for the power the *Star-Telegram* enjoyed in West Texas. The Lubbock editors assigned me to cover a big murder trial in Littlefield in 1953. I was welcomed by the judge, the prosecutors, and defense attorneys. I felt special until the late George Dolan showed up to cover the trial for the *Star-Telegram*.

George was renowned throughout West Texas, thanks to his front-page column entitled "This Is West Texas." Suddenly judge and attorneys fell all over themselves offering to assist George. He was definitely king of the hill. As the reporter from nearby Lubbock, I no longer was entitled to such a lofty position.

I worked for the *Morning Avalanche*. My fellow reporters and I toiled until 2 a.m. Even though I was well aware of how the *Star-Telegram* covered the area, I still would be amazed to see the newspaper being delivered home-to-home before the Lubbock paper.

On one occasion I was dispatched to cover a visit to New Mexico by that state's governor. Again I was amazed to find that the largest sign on that western New Mexico city's main street was that of the *Star-Telegram* distributor.

My employment in Lubbock was interrupted for two years when I was drafted into the army for the Korean conflict, which broke out the day I reported for work. I had spent nearly a year and a half in Lubbock. It had been a great learning experience under the guidance of crusty night editor Jay Harris.

I was summoned back to the *Star-Telegram* in January 1950. I always regretted that Mr. Record did not live long enough to see me named managing editor of the morning and evening editions. I retired from the newspaper the last day of 1997. The paper—and West Texas—will forever remain a part of me.

Veteran Austin journalist Sam Kinch Jr., whose father had been Austin bureau chief for the *Star-Telegram*, attributed the newspaper's domination of West Texas during much of the twentieth century to six factors:

the "Fort Worth—Where the West Begins" trademark of the *Star-Telegram* was justified by the paper's circulation in as many as 84 West Texas counties. Six factors contributed to the *Star-Telegram*'s prominence in West Texas: (1) during "bargain days" in each October, November and December, yearly subscriptions to the paper were sold at reduced rates; (2) the *Star-Telegram* hired hundreds of "stringer" reporters in cities and towns all over West Texas; (3) transportation facilities were available and efficient to circulation distribution points; (4) as many as 13 editions of the paper were published to coincide with transportation and circulation factors; (5) the *Star-Telegram* devoted a great deal of space to news of West Texas interest, such as local politics, chambers of commerce, oil and gas, sports, agriculture, livestock, water, etc.; (5) the paper covered several stories of interest to West Texas more adequately than any other news medium.[3]

The newspaper was delivered to cities, towns, and villages throughout West Texas by truck, bus, and train. But trains were key to the system. Fort Worth was a railroad hub. Trains headed west at night would have mail cars loaded with bundles of the newspaper. They would be dropped off at every stop. Individual dealers would then deliver them to nearby homes and remote ranches.

The *Star-Telegram* would go to extremes to get the news to West Texans. Phillip J. Meek, president and editorial chairman of the newspaper, recalled one such case in a 1981 speech when the paper was honored on its seventy-fifth anniversary by The Newcomer Society of North America.

Later, when American Airlines established its Fort Worth–to–Los Angeles route, the pilot of the old Ford tri-motor would fly down low over a spread near Guadalupe Peak and pitch out a bundle of *Star-Telegram*s to ranchers whose homes were at least 60 miles from the nearest town. For almost half a century, the *Star-Telegram* was the one newspaper that catered exclusively to the scattered towns and ranches along the Caprock, across the staked plains and on a stretch of barren countryside that *Star-Telegram* editors refused to call either desert or wasteland.[4]

How right he was. The newspaper could find ways to put a positive spin on the worst of news. There was a standing joke in the Fort Worth office that if West Texas was devastated by floods, the banner on the next day's *Star-Telegram* would probably read:

BENEFICIAL FLOODS CLAIM
FOUR LIVES IN WEST TEXAS

James R. Record would have nodded approval.

Record had a fixation about weather, especially rain. State correspondents were paid a dollar to call in rain reports. Whenever it rained anywhere in West Texas, the newspaper would run a long chart reporting even the smallest of downfalls in remote areas to the west. And woe to the city editor who could not inform Mr. Record about how much it had rained the previous night on his family ranch in Throckmorton.

Correspondents also were kept busy filing obituaries. Some were hilarious. I recall one that broke us up while I was working on the morning edition copydesk in the 1950s. The veteran female stringer got carried away when reporting the death of a prominent clubwoman in her town. The woman, the correspondent noted in her opening paragraph, had been "wafted away on the wings of angels." That didn't fly in the *Star-Telegram*. Nor did they "pass away." They simply "died."

Carter never hesitated to use his political clout or the power of his newspaper to win favors for Fort Worth and West Texas.

Texas Tech University owes its existence to Carter and the newspaper.[5] As did other projects. As Flemmons reports:

If Haskell township needed federal funds for a new hospital, city fathers jumped into their old pickups, drove to Fort Worth and laid their problem on his desk. A postmaster's position for Sonora? Candidates applied to Amon Carter. A state park for Monahans? New roads for Tulia? No problem. Amon Carter could do it, and did.[6]

Many newspaper syndicates conceded that West Texas was *Star-Telegram* territory and granted the newspaper exclusive rights to some of the most popular features, especially comic strips, in the vast area. For many years, if West Texans wanted to follow the adventures of Dick Tracy, they had to purchase the *Star-Telegram*.

The newspaper devoted many news columns and personnel to covering oil, farming, and ranching. At least three reporters were assigned to developments in the oil industry. New staff members were warned never to touch the oil writer Royce Yancy's map rack. It contained maps pinpointing the status of every well drilled in West Texas. A minimum of three reporters covered the farm and ranch business. One, veteran Frank Reeves, roamed the ranges for such long stretches that he was a virtual stranger when he visited the newsroom.

Friday nights in the fall called for maximum staff effort as the newspaper covered the king of West Texas sports—high school football. Reporters who were assigned to cover the police, the courthouse, and city hall during the week were dispatched to cities and towns throughout West Texas to cover games. Their wives and sisters and girlfriends were hired to work in the downtown Fort Worth office to take game accounts phoned in by staff members and correspondents. It was a madhouse.

And it could be chilling. I remember when I was sent to Childress one late November night to cover a playoff game involving a couple of far West Texas powerhouses. It had been a warm day, and I wore only a light jacket in a press box that had no heat or protective window. An infamous norther blew in out of the Panhandle the moment of kickoff.

Never have I been so cold. Some subzero days at Notre Dame could not match what I was enduring. I could not type. I did manage to take some notes in pencil.

After the game, a genial hotel clerk in downtown Childress permitted me to sit in the warm lobby to type my story. I then walked next door and handed it to a Western Union operator, who dispatched it directly to the Fort Worth newsroom.

The next day, many of us again would be recruited by the sports department to help cover Southwest Conference football games. Up to six reporters and photographers would be assigned to a game. West Texans had a thirst for football, and the *Star-Telegram* wanted to make sure it quenched that thirst.

West Texans would give these representatives of the newspaper the royal treatment. Remember how I had had to play second fiddle to George Dolan while covering the murder trial in Littlefield? As a *Star-Telegram* reporter, I learned what it was like to be Number One.

I recall when I was assigned to cover a sensational murder trial in Cisco in 1963. By then, the newspaper was encountering stiff competition in the region. In this instance, it was a staffer from the *Abilene Reporter-News*. As soon as I arrived at the courthouse, I was greeted by District Judge Bill Oxford, who had enjoyed the newspaper's endorsement in the past. When I told him I needed private working space, he turned his office over to me. The reporter from Abilene had to make do on a wooden bench in the hallway.

Whenever I needed to take a break to call in an update of my story for the next edition, I merely gave Judge Oxford a time-out signal, and he would immediately call a recess until I had completed my phone call. It was then that I came to realize why recesses at that Littlefield trial had always seemed to happen just when Dolan needed to call in an update.

The *Star-Telegram* began losing its firm grip on West Texas in the 1950s. Several things contributed to this.

Train service declined. No longer were mail cars filled with bundles of the newspaper stopping at every small town that merited a population sign from the highway department. Truck and bus service was not a suitable substitute.

Local newspapers in such places as Amarillo, Lubbock, Wichita Falls, San Angelo, Midland, and Abilene were becoming more aggressive in covering surrounding counties. They cut into the *Star-Telegram*'s circulation because they could provide their home folks, farmers, and ranchers more local news in a more timely fashion than could their rival in Fort Worth.

Newspaper syndicates no longer considered West Texas the exclusive kingdom of the *Star-Telegram* and did not renew many of its contracts for exclusive rights to popular features. Comics and cartoons once found only in the paper from Fort Worth now appeared in papers throughout West Texas.

The Associated Press extended its wire photo and stock market services into far West Texas, making it possible for regional papers to provide more timely coverage.

The *Star-Telegram* began to cut off service deliberately to far reaches of West Texas and eastern New Mexico. Declining circulation meant it did not make good financial sense to service these areas.

The withdrawal drew strong protest from readers who had grown up on the newspaper.

Finally, in the late 1980s, the *Star-Telegram*'s primary West Texas circulation area ran from Hillsboro to Abilene to Wichita Falls, still a sizeable area.

Today, when I visit friends in Lubbock and Midland and my links to the *Star-Telegram* are made known, I get protests from old-timers because they can't get the paper on a timely basis. When I try to explain that their own local paper can give them better and quicker service now, they are apt to reply: "You just don't get it. I grew up in a home where the *Star-Telegram* and the Bible were always on the table in the living room."

PHIL RECORD, *a native of Fort Worth, spent most of his professional career at the Fort Worth Star-Telegram. He served in many positions, from copyboy to associate executive editor. He retired at the end of 1997 after serving as the newspaper's first ombudsman. He currently is a professional in residence at Texas Christian University, where he teaches media ethics.*

NOTES

1. Jerry Flemmons, Amon: The Life of Amon Carter, Sr., of Texas (Austin: Jenkins, 1978), 99.
2. Ibid., 27.
3. Sam Kinch Jr., "Amon Carter: Publisher-Salesman" (master's thesis, University of Texas at Austin, 1965), 12.
4. Phillip J. Meek, published speech at the Fort Worth Club (February 26, 1981), 13.
5. Flemmons, *Amon*, 281.
6. Ibid., 21.

CHAPTER 7

Prying Open Public Access

TONY PEDERSON

Scandal always has had a way of stimulating change, even in difficult and slow-moving legislative environments. In Texas, it took a whopper of a scandal to create the state's basic open government laws that we have today. The Sharpstown scandal of 1971 was just that, and more.

Frank Sharp of Houston was the typical wheeler-dealer businessman of the era. He had made loans of more than $600,000 from his Sharpstown State Bank to a number of state officials for stock purchases in one of his companies, National Bankers Life Insurance Corporation. Sharp manipulated the stock price so that the officials sold the stock back at handsome profits. The idea was a straightforward proposition in order to grease the way for passage of state legislation favorable to his bank. That occurred in a special session of the Texas legislature in 1969. The scheme was a rather clumsy one that was easily tracked. Just as the 1971 session of the legislature was cranking up, the Securities and Exchange Commission filed a stock-fraud suit in federal court in Dallas detailing the transactions.

Before it was over, Texas House Speaker Gus Mutscher, one of his key aides, and a state representative were indicted and convicted. The three were tried in Abilene and became known as the "Abilene Three." In typical Texas fashion, however, none of the three went to jail, nor did Sharp. All received probation, and Sharp paid a $5,000 fine after being granted immunity for his testimony. (The only one to serve time over the Sharpstown scandal was John Osorio, former state insurance commissioner, who served fourteen months. He later would regain his law license and practice law. In what might be thought of as another stroke of Texas justice, in 2000 Osorio and a lady friend would claim the winning ticket to a $60 million jackpot in the Texas Lottery.)

Numerous others, including Governor Preston Smith, Lieutenant Governor Ben Barnes, and Attorney General Waggoner Carr, were implicated and saw their political careers ruined. Upon Smith's death in 2003, newspaper obituaries across the state mentioned his polka-dot ties and his downfall because of Sharpstown. Smith had taken a loan from Sharp and ended up splitting a quick profit of $125,000 with his investment partner, state Democratic chairman Dr. Elmer Baum. Smith contended he had done nothing wrong because he had been unaware of Sharp's interest in the banking bills passed in the special session. Though he was responsible for the legislature getting the two Sharp bills in the first place, Smith vetoed the bills on the advice of his aides. Though Smith was never charged, the damage was done, and the perception remained that the state's highest elected official had been a part of the scandal. Smith sought reelection in 1972 but finished a dismal fourth in the Democratic primary.

The voters of Texas were appropriately angered. Half of the House and Senate members of 1971 did not return for the 63rd Legislature in 1973, either by deciding not to run or by losing elections. A reform-minded legislature was elected in 1972, setting the stage for major changes in the way business was done in Texas. The legislature passed ethics changes mandating the reporting of income and election finances by state candidates as well as the disclosure of lobbyists' activities. The centerpieces of the reforms were the Texas Open Meetings Act and the Texas Open Records Act.

Throughout the 1960s, the so-called sunshine laws had gained popularity and were being routinely enacted by states. Florida had first passed an open records act in 1909. The first federal Freedom of Information Act was passed in 1966 and signed by President Johnson. Texas no doubt would have adopted similar sunshine laws sooner or later, but anger from the public helped fuel the atmosphere for passage.

Don Adams, who went on to become a well-known lobbyist in Austin, was elected to the House of Representatives from Jasper in 1968. He was elected to the Senate in 1972, and co-sponsored both the Open Records Act and the Open Meetings Act in the 1973 session. He had served in the House during the 1971 session that had been virtually paralyzed by the anger, both from the public and inside the legislature, over the Sharpstown scandal. Even though Adams had voted against the bills sought by Sharp and managed to win a Senate seat, he felt the resentment from public opinion.

"Having voted against the bills was no immunity. If you were in Austin you were part of the problem," Adams said. "I have never seen the public in such an angry mood. And of course in 1971, the mood in the House was sharply divided because of Gus. It was the House liberals against the conservatives, and the liberals wanted an investigation of Gus."

To understand how the Open Records Act came about in 1973, one must first understand the poisonous atmosphere that existed in the 1971 legislature after the Sharpstown scandal erupted. There were only a handful of Republicans in the legislature in those days, but the Democrats were in two firmly entrenched camps. Adams described the action as "Democrats eating Democrats." In *Texas under a Cloud,* published in 1972, Sam Kinch Jr. and Ben Procter wrote, "Lest there be any mistake in historical perspective, in early February, 1971, the entire tone of Texas politics was one of crisis." The *Fort Worth Star-Telegram* would later refer to the 62nd Legislature as a "scandalous debacle." John Hill, who was elected attorney general in 1972 and later became chief justice of the Texas Supreme Court, put it this way: "Sometimes you can do just about anything to people up to the point of embarrassing them. With the Sharpstown scandal and what happened after that, the people of the state of Texas were embarrassed."

Sharpstown was just one sign of what people generally and correctly assumed to be a corrupt and broken system of good ol' boys in Austin. Tales of backroom dealings, bribes—some involving money and some quid pro quo—and all nature of high jinks and shenanigans had circulated for years and were well known both to the public and to government officials. The lobbyists wielded enormous power, often gaining a free hand in writing legislation. And of course virtually everything—from the womanizing to writing the state budget—occurred in secret. There had actually been an open-meetings act passed by the legislature in 1967, but it was so full of holes and so lacking in enforcement authority that it was routinely ignored. And the legislature had been thoughtful enough to include an exemption for itself, allowing virtually the entire legislative process to proceed without meaningful scrutiny.

"In terms of the legislative environment before Sharpstown, the context was always that the business interests and the political interests were exactly the same," says Kinch, who in the 1970s was an Austin bureau reporter and columnist for the *Dallas Morning News.* "Business was always in charge, and everything came from the top."

And then came the 1973 session with a new speaker of the House, Price Daniel Jr., and a new lieutenant governor presiding over the Senate, Bill Hobby. Interestingly, both had newspaper connections. Daniel's family owned a small newspaper in Liberty. Before his election, Bill Hobby was executive editor of the *Houston Post,* which his family owned. Both Hobby and Daniel set aggressive agendas for reform, even though there would be disagreements between them. Daniel had his reform bills flying out of the House early in the session, often without sufficient debate or hearings, and then would blame Hobby for not handling the bills in an expeditious fashion. "The bills

Don Adams (l) and William P. Hobby Jr. (r) in the Texas State Legislature,
1973. *Courtesy of The Senate of The State of Texas, Media Services.*

left the House without the proper study or consideration as to their content
and their impact," Hobby says of the conflict during the session. "When the
bills got to the Senate, they got that type of consideration. That's what the
Senate is for."

Hobby had put the open-records and open-meetings bills on his personal
agenda for the Senate. "There was just never any question in my mind that
everything, every part of government, had to be completely transparent,"
Hobby says. "And I haven't changed my opinion on that. Everything should be
transparent today, including, in my opinion, newspapers." Hobby remembers
a few "dinosaurs" in the legislature who opposed the bills, but the legislation
passed with relative ease, and both the open-meetings and open-records bills
were signed into law by newly elected governor, Dolph Briscoe.

Though the reform-minded legislature left little doubt that major changes
would be made in state government, there was by no means unanimous public
support for some of the changes, including the sunshine laws. Adams recalls
getting a call from a woman who served on a local school board.

"She said, 'I really want you to vote against those two bills,'" Adams
recalls. "I said, 'I can't do that. I'm one of the sponsors.' She said, 'Can you
imagine what kind of pressure we'd be under if we were voting on teacher
salaries and bond issues if the press was there reporting on it?' And I said,
'Don't you think the public has an interest in what you're voting on?' She
said she didn't think the public was really that interested. I got another call
from a county commissioner and he said just about the same thing. To me it

was pretty amazing. It was obvious that the politicians preferred to do things in the dead of night so they wouldn't have to take the heat for decisions they made. It's interesting that the only calls I got on the two bills were calls from people in opposition."

Opposition by public schools was predictable. One lobbyist for the Texas Association of School Boards called the original bill "an atrocity," adding that it provided for the "criminalization of normal social events." William Boykin, who was head of the Texas Press Association at the time, had just come to Texas from Florida. He remembers offering testimony in favor of the open-records and open-meetings bills before a Senate committee and being called a "Florida Communist" by one of the senators.

The bills that were passed by the House and Senate and signed by Governor Briscoe were more or less standard sunshine bills, hardly aggressive in their nature, but both made enormous strides toward openness. The open-meetings bill ended up being watered down somewhat in the Senate when a committee expanded the provisions under which closed meetings could take place. Nevertheless, the final bill mandated open meetings for every governmental body, including state agencies, boards, and commissions and, yes, legislative committees. A "meeting" was defined, and public notice of seventy-two hours was specified. The final bill also included penalties for violating the act: a fine of up to $500 and a jail term of one to six months.

The Open Records Act contained an elegant preamble, preserved to this day, regarding the need of the public to have information for self-governance. The preamble says, in part, "The people, in delegating authority, do not give their public servants the right to decide what is good for the people to know and what is not good for them to know. The people insist on remaining informed so that they may retain control over the instruments they have created." The preamble concludes with the forceful declaration that the provisions of the law are to be "liberally construed" in order to carry out the policy.

The exact role of Texas newspapers in passing the laws for open records and open meetings is difficult to ascertain. Certainly the extensive publicity of the Sharpstown scandal, especially by the larger newspapers with staffs in Austin, helped set the agenda for change and convinced the public that things were not right in the state capital. There was also consistent editorial writing in papers across the state, a unified voice calling not only for more openness in the legislative process but also for overall change in the legislative atmosphere. Kinch probably gets it right when he says that newspapers in Texas cannot be directly credited with passing the bills. "But," Kinch says, now after thirty years of perspective, "I think it can be said that the Open

Records Act and the Open Meetings Act wouldn't have been passed without the newspapers."

There are plenty of reporters from earlier days who claim that the current open-government laws, particularly the Public Information Act, impede more than help access to information. It is true that there was a time when reporters basically got all the information they wanted directly from government officials. The officials themselves were much more accessible and, often, openly friendly with journalists. Information generally was available for the asking and usually complete.

Time and events have changed that relationship. Longtime journalism professor David McHam, a reporter in Houston in the 1960s, is not certain exactly why the relationship changed. "Maybe it was Vietnam," McHam says. "For sure things changed after Watergate." In any case, government officials became more and more hostile to journalists, and journalists became more skeptical and critical of government and officials.

In 1989, longtime *Houston Post* Austin reporter Felton West wrote a column bemoaning the bureaucracy, expense, and time necessary to get public records. He went on at length about how, before the state's Open Records Act, a reporter could simply call up a government office, request information, and get it. West noted, correctly, that after passage of the Open Records Act, virtually any request for even routine information had to be made in writing, which set in motion the formal and legal process for review. The law called for a governmental agency to respond within ten days, and it became customary for the agency to wait exactly ten days before reporting to the requestor whether the information was considered public or not. Then, there was the time needed to gather and copy the documents. On top of that, there came to be associated with routine requests charges, often exorbitant, for reviewing the documents for privacy matters, copying, and, if needed, redacting information that was deemed private.

West closed his column with a particular horror story. "The other day an *Austin American-Statesman* reporter called up Ben Ellis, the mayor of the suburban Village of Garfield, and asked for the names of the candidates who had filed for mayor and aldermen in the village's election," West wrote. "Ellis refused to furnish the names, saying the newspaper would have to make a written request for them under the Open Records Act before he would. My God, how far have we regressed? If it's that difficult for a reporter to pry out information about the village election, I can only wonder how much trouble ordinary taxpaying citizens have."

Now, more than 30 years after the passage of the acts, West is in agreement that the laws have overall served Texas well, despite shortcomings, exemptions, and assorted other issues. "The laws have been a tool that has helped to produce a lot of openness that otherwise we wouldn't have had," he says.

Despite its problems and growing list of exemptions, the Texas Open Records Act has persisted and proved for the most part adequate. With increasing computerization of records in the late 1980s and early 1990s, however, new problems developed regarding access. Governmental agencies began charging for computer time in addition to normal copying fees. It was not infrequent for agencies to claim that the records did not exist in the form requested; the substantial fees for developing the programs necessary to retrieve the documents were passed on to requestors.

In 1995, the Texas Open Records Act was rewritten to become the Texas Public Information Act. The new law took into account computerization and new ways to access data. It also was more specific in promoting reasonable charges. It was a bill that was almost dead on at least a dozen occasions during the session. The House sponsor, Representative Sylvester Turner of Houston, had faced withering criticism from some of his colleagues who were acting on behalf of Texas municipalities. Local governments claimed that the bill was too burdensome and would dramatically increase the costs of open government while limiting the recovery of fees. The bill finally passed the House and, late in the session in May, died again in a conference committee.

Acting at the behest of Texas newspapers and a combined lobbying effort by the Texas Press Association and the Texas Daily Newspaper Association, Lieutenant Governor Bob Bullock revived the bill, specifically dictated the final compromise language, and railroaded it through the final approval process. In many respects, it was typical Bullock. As cantankerous and even ill-tempered as he could be on occasion, he generally acted in the best interest of Texas. And nothing less than an ill-tempered rage could have gotten the measure passed in 1995. The Texas Public Information Act, though not perfect, has generally served the public and freedom of information well in the years since its adoption.

Long before the fight over open records and open meetings, Texas newspapers had lobbied for uniform procedures for the posting of legal notices. *A History of the Texas Press Association* published in 1916 notes that the organization had discussed legal advertising at every one of its annual conventions, ever since the TPA was founded in 1880. The effort had picked up momentum in the early part of the twentieth century: the TPA history noted that a full report had been presented to the annual convention in San Antonio in 1913. The newspapers took the position that, in the case of property posted for sale in debtor cases, fairness dictated the widest possible distribution of information about the sales. As the early TPA history notes,

> The unfortunate debtor continues to see his property sold at a sacrifice at forced sale and without advertising other than on bulletin boards, trees, and out of the way places which few see or read—a custom that has survived the days when newspapers were few and far between.

It was no doubt a valid point, but legislators generally expressed the feeling that the newspaper lobbying efforts were more dictated by self-interest in securing more advertising dollars than in any spirit of public service. The feeling has continued to this day. Newspapers' lobbying for freedom of information is still viewed with some skepticism and frequent accusations that the motive is profit rather than serving the public good.

The newspaper effort eventually paid off, and in the 1920s a series of bills passed requiring that legal advertising be published in general-circulation newspapers. The rate for legal advertising was set as the lowest rate the newspaper charged for classified advertising. In recent years, legal advertising has become controversial again, as proposals have been made to allow legal-notice advertising over the Internet, thereby reducing costs for governmental agencies and cutting out newspapers entirely. The Internet proposals have not been received well in Texas so far, but it can be assumed that such bills will continue to be filed and considered.

The sunshine laws in all states were created for the public to have access to governmental processes. The media have been particular beneficiaries, ostensibly acting on behalf of the public. But newspapers themselves have played a special role in litigating matters related to open government. For the most part, the public can't afford the costs of pursuing resolutions through the legal process. Because of their resources, the larger newspapers in Texas have been the leaders in expanding access by litigation based on the open-government laws.

A key controversy over the Open Records Act erupted almost immediately after its passage in 1973. The Houston Police Department took the position that police offense reports were not included in the Open Records Act and that only limited information should be made public. The *Houston Chronicle* had sought the information on the offense reports as well as personal histories of suspects and administrative records. The department further decided that reporters could not actually examine the offense reports, even though they had routinely been available for inspection in the past. Attorney General John

Hill initially sided with the police department on the issue, but later changed his mind, issuing an opinion that granted limited access to the records.

The *Chronicle* sued, seeking a declaratory judgment that the Open Records Act established a right of access to all three types of documents. The *Chronicle* won in the 1st Court of Appeals in Houston in a 1975 decision, *Houston Chronicle Publishing Company v. City of Houston*, gaining access to the offense reports and administrative records but not the personal histories and individual arrest records. Hill later issued an opinion specifically setting out the public access as determined by the appeals court. The case is now referred to as *Chronicle I*, setting it apart from a later *Chronicle II*, a lawsuit also against the City of Houston in the 1980s that sought and gained information regarding prisoners detained in the Houston City Jail.

In the early 1980s, the *Bryan–College Station Eagle* challenged the openness of the process by which Texas A&M University selected its president. The paper sought the names and qualifications of candidates for the position. In *Hubert v. Harte-Hanks Texas Newspapers, Inc.* (1988), the court of appeals in Austin rejected the notion that the process must be kept secret in order to encourage candidates to apply. The legislature then passed a law allowing public universities to disclose information about "finalists." Predictably, universities have been announcing only one "finalist" in candidate searches since then. Nonetheless, there has frequently been debate about the qualifications of the one finalist, and this case also helped force disclosure of information regarding searches for city managers, school superintendents, and other positions selected by governmental bodies.

In 1986, in *Board of Trustees v. Cox Enterprises, Inc.*, the *Austin American-Statesman*, after a lengthy battle with the Austin Independent School District, gained clarification of a number of issues relating to the Open Meetings Act. The Texas Supreme Court clarified specific requirements for what constitutes notice of a meeting and the need to specify the subjects to be discussed, even those subjects considered in executive session. The court also said that before an executive session could take place, the board had to have a quorum present and to meet publicly before the executive session. Finally, the court ruled that holding a "straw poll" in executive session and then announcing it in a public meeting was not permitted. This case has provided important guidelines for how public meetings must be conducted in Texas.

One of the most significant open-records cases in Texas dealing with crime information resulted in the *Fort Worth Star-Telegram* winning two decisions in the Texas Supreme Court over reporting on a rape case. The *Star-Telegram*, without publishing the name of the rape victim, published her age and other information about her: she owned a travel agency, lived on the east side of Fort Worth, and drove a black Jaguar (which had been stolen and was being used by the suspect when he was arrested). The woman sued, claiming that the newspaper had published enough information to identify her and had invaded her privacy. The trial judge issued a protective order prohibiting the *Star-Telegram* from disclosing her real name.

The paper had no intention of publishing her real name, but sought a writ of mandamus to remove the prior restraint on publication. Eventually, the Texas Supreme Court granted relief (*Star-Telegram, Inc. v. Walker*, 1992), saying that the protective order "unreasonably restricts expression by preventing the dissemination of public information." As to the initial privacy suit, the judge granted summary judgment in favor of the newspaper. The woman appealed, but the Texas Supreme Court ruled in favor of the *Star-Telegram* (*Star-Telegram, Inc. v. Doe*, 1995), saying that it "would be impossible to require (the media) to avoid every conceivable circumstance where a party might be subjected to the stress of some unpleasant or undesired notoriety without an unacceptable chilling effect on the media itself."

Another *Houston Chronicle* case, this one a privacy suit brought by a prisoner in the Texas Department of Corrections, resulted in the Texas Supreme Court rejecting the "false light" doctrine as a means of action in the state. Clyde Ura Cain was a convicted murderer, burglar, pimp, and thief. The *Chronicle* had pointed out all this, and also claimed that Cain was a member of a racist prison gang known as the "Dixie Mafia." Cain claimed that calling him a member of the Dixie Mafia put him in a false light and entitled him to damages. In *Cain v. Hearst Corp.* (1994), the court rejected the claim of privacy invasion based on "false light" because it substantially duplicates other forms of recovery, mainly libel, and because it lacks safeguards against frivolous claims, thereby chilling protected speech by imposing an impermissibly vague standard of liability.

Texas is now among the minority of states that have no shield law to protect the identity of confidential sources. Challenges to subpoenas to disclose sources have been fought by many media organizations, with mixed success. The *Dallas Morning News*, in a 1991 libel suit filed by Sheriff Gene Falcon of Starr County, gained a successful ruling on protecting sources as a part of libel litigation. The paper had published a story regarding murder charges against the sheriff and linking him to drug trafficking. The court of appeals in San Antonio sided with the paper, ruling that a privilege existed and could be overcome only if the sheriff proved that statements made about him were materially false and that evidence about him was not available by other means.

It would stand to reason that, Texas being Texas, college football would produce litigation. The *Fort Worth Star-Telegram* sued Texas A&M during the height of some of the recruiting scandals in the 1980s. In *Vandiver v. Star-Telegram, Inc.* (1988), the Austin court of appeals ruled for the newspaper, holding that neither privacy concerns nor the Buckley Amendment (a federal law governing the confidentiality of educational information) prevented the release of information about recruiting violations.

One of the most ambitious legislative projects undertaken by newspapers involved obtaining a change in Texas law to allow interlocutory appeal (an appeal that occurs while a trial is in progress, rather than after a verdict has been rendered) of the denial of summary judgment in libel cases. In the early 1990s, a $57 million verdict against WFAA-TV in a case brought by Waco district attorney Vic Feazell and a $31 million verdict won by a heart surgeon against KENS-TV in San Antonio spurred the effort. Belo Corporation, owner of WFAA-TV and the *Dallas Morning News*, led the campaign and the coordination among Texas newspapers and broadcasters. Paul Watler of the Dallas law firm Jenkens & Gilchrist wrote the new statute and provided the legal guidance for the change. Studies have consistently shown that even though media defendants ultimately prevail in the vast majority of libel cases, they generally lose at the trial level. The change allows appellate review of cases that often are frivolous and without merit.

In recent years, newspapers as well as open-government advocates such as the Freedom of Information Foundation of Texas (FOIFT) have begun working closely with the Texas attorney general's office. The attorney routinely issues opinions when governmental agencies seek guidance on whether or not to release records. It became common for the agencies to seek such opinions as a means of delaying the release of what obviously were public documents. Recent attorneys general have recognized this abuse for what it is and have been willing to deal more aggressively with agencies.

Newspapers' relationships with attorneys general in Texas have had their ups and downs—have even been downright difficult at times—but in recent years that has not been the case. Working with lawyers from the FOIFT, most of whom represent the major media organizations in the state, the attorney general's office has streamlined the opinion process and has been more inclined toward ordering the disclosure of documents. Additionally, enforcement on open-meetings abuses has been more aggressive, and the prosecution of public officials has become, if not routine, at least frequent enough to provide a realistic threat to those wanting to circumvent the Open Meetings Act.

Though newspapers have continued to fight the perception of both the public and the legislature that their interests in openness are commercial, the fact remains that significant gains in freedom of information and access to government have been obtained through the efforts of Texas newspapers.

TONY PEDERSON *is a professor at Southern Methodist University in Dallas, where he occupies the Belo Distinguished Chair in Journalism. He worked for twenty-nine years for the* Houston Chronicle *and was senior vice president and executive editor before retiring in 2003. He is a native of Waco and a graduate of Baylor University. He holds a master's degree in journalism from Ohio State University.*

CHAPTER 8

Woman's Work

SARAH L. GREENE

Women's role in the development of Texas community newspapers is not fully reflected in the annals of the Texas Press Association. It has been significant, nevertheless.

Until late in the twentieth century, many weekly newspapers were family operations in which publishers' wives filled every conceivable position. Not unusual was Mrs. L. B. Smith, wife of the publisher of the *Brady Standard*.

"As my husband's helpmate, I fill in the gap automatically when an opening develops—like when he loses a society editor, a bookkeeper, an ad salesman, or a general all-around handyman," she said in 1957.[1]

For three decades after the TPA was organized in 1880, women attended conventions with their husbands, as indicated by group photographs. With a few exceptions, such as when filling the position of "poetess," they were seen but not heard. The notable TPA railroad excursion to San Francisco in 1882 was for men only.[2]

In 1889, however, eight "ladies of the Texas Press Association" were invited to go on the postconvention railroad excursion to Mexico City. In turn, the distaff travelers passed a resolution expressing thanks for "the chivalric devotion and unfailing attention" that had been given them by the men on the trip, who had proven to be "true and courteous gentlemen." The resolution was signed by Miss Ruth Cook and seven married women identified only by "Mrs." in front of their husbands' names—a style that continued through at least three-quarters of the twentieth century.[3]

At the 1893 TPA convention in Dallas, Aurelia Hadley Mohl, editor of the "Woman's World" department at the *Houston Post*, announced that "ladies engaged in journalist and literary work" would meet to organize a press association of their own, the Texas Woman's Press Association.

Perry Hawkins of the *Taylor Journal*, speaking on women in journalism, tried to discourage this movement. He asserted approvingly "their presence at the conventions of the men had a tendency to banish wine from the banquets."

Hawkins "referred very tenderly and lovingly to the ladies and said they had proved a success in everything they had so far attempted, and the field of journalism was no exception." He did not believe they had received the encouragement their abilities deserved.[4]

Mrs. Mohl was not deterred. At that time women members of the TPA were relegated to the balcony as spectators, and she was determined to bring them to the main floor.

FROM SIDEKICK TO MADAME PRESIDENT
MARY HENKEL JUDSON

C. M. "Cap" Henkel Jr. left the merchant marine after World War II and moved to Groves, where he and the late Farris Block started the *Mid-County Review*.

Farris later became head of public information at the University of Houston and was active in the Texas Gulf Coast Press Association.

Cap had no prior newspaper experience; he was just full of opinions, well traveled and well read. He and Farris sat back to back and tapped out opposing editorials: Cap from the far right, Farris from the far left. They were friends to the end.

In 1955, Cap moved to Robstown to become news editor for the late Carroll Keach at the *Robstown Record*. There he led his first-grade daughter, whom he called Miss Red, around town, taking pictures when the eye of Hurricane Carla passed over in 1961. That is my first memory of Cap as a newspaperman and me as his sidekick.

In 1963, Cap became publisher of the *Refugio County Press*. He waged many successful campaigns during his thirteen years in Refugio. Throughout Cap's tenure in Refugio, his editor and faithful companion, as well as the mother of his five children, was his wife, Kitty.

Cap officially introduced me to the newspaper business when I was in the fifth grade. That was in 1964, when he put me to working writing the "Junior Beat" column, which contained news of junior high school students. I filled in occasionally, helped out with circulation, and eventually graduated to writing the high school gossip column.

Vowing never to go into the newspaper business, I went off to college to major in English, with no clue of what I would do with such a degree. After my freshman year I came home for the summer, and Cap put me to work writing feature stories, running the Thursday morning route throughout Refugio County, and taking photos. One of my photos won an honorable mention in the National Newspaper Association's contest that year.

Cap had set the bait and I was hooked.

I returned to Southwest Texas State University to major in journalism and minor in partying. The following semester found me at Texas A&I University in Kingsville, where I lived under the supervision of my brother and sister-in-law and dropped my minor. I finally enrolled at the University of Texas at Austin, where I originally

In a tandem effort on the same day, May 10, 1893, Mrs. Mohl attended another meeting at which she helped found the Texas Equal Rights Association. For the next three decades, the support of suffrage absorbed the creative energies of the Houston writer and other Texas women.[5]

Women's participation at TPA meetings was typically limited to reading a commentary or reciting poems. But most used the opportunity to assert the undeniable female influence on community newspapers.

Mrs. Julia Truitt Bishop of Austin, speaking on "Women in Journalism" at the 1893 TPA meeting, said, "While women are, perhaps, not practical enough to meet the demands of modern newspapers, they have brought to

---

had been accepted but had not attended because Cap did not want me associating with all the hippies there (including one of my brothers). At UT, I had the privilege of taking classes under Griff Singer and the late Martin L. "Red" Gibson.

In the summer of 1974 I landed an internship at the *Corpus Christi Caller-Times*, and it was there that I met Murray, who was a photographer for the *Caller*.

I returned to UT in the fall and, like Walter Cronkite, dropped out of UT midway through that semester. I'm not sure why he did, but I did because of debilitating allergies.

Out of the Hill Country and back on the South Texas plains, I went to work for the late Jim Tracy in Sinton at the *San Patricio County News*, where I covered city, school, county, and general assignments. Although sports was not, and is not, my forte, I even filled in as sportswriter when Jim Jr. was hospitalized with a heart ailment.

When Murray and I announced our engagement in 1975, my parents found it convenient to retire. Their positions were offered to us, altered to accommodate the differences in our areas of concentration. So in the spring of 1976, after we married, Murray and I went to work at the *Refugio County Press*.

In 1981, we purchased the *Port Aransas South Jetty*, and the next year we bought the *Refugio County Press* from the thirty-five stockholders who had started the paper in 1959.

We moved to Port Aransas in 1983, and in 1988 we sold the *Refugio County Press*. In the meantime we were partners for a short time in the *Goliad Advance Guard* and a free circulation publication called *ENTERTAINMENT!*

Active in the TPA, the South Texas Press Association, and the Texas Gulf Coast Press Association, I was president of the STPA in 1979–1980, president of the TPA in 1990–1991, and president of the TGCPA in 1994–1995.

When Fred Barbee was TPA president—I believe in 1977—he appointed me to the TPA board, and I stayed there until they made me president to get rid of me.

MARY HENKEL JUDSON is publisher of *Port Aransas South Jetty*. She was the first woman president of the Texas Press Association (1990–1991). In 2004 she was assistant to the president of the STPA and a director for the TGCPA.

those newspapers something they sadly needed—a touch of heartfelt tender-ness to the hard utilitarianism of the age."

Mrs. C. Bryarly of the *Center Star-News* was another convention stalwart and regular attendee, but perhaps because of the press of business, sent in her commentary on "The Country Editor's Wife" to be read at the 1894 meeting in Fort Worth.

Mrs. Fred B. Robinson echoed that topic at the 1896 convention in El Paso, speaking on "An Editor's Wife on the Pay Roll." It's likely she was speaking metaphorically, for wives and children were most often unpaid workers in the family newspaper business.[6]

The post–Civil War era dominated by individualistic, fiery editor-publishers who "spiked printers ink with vitriol" was not over, but change was in the air. The new, twentieth-century newspaper office became a more woman-friendly place—unless a woman was confronted with learning the amazing Linotype machine that replaced hand-set type.[7]

Mrs. Burton Fielder (of the *Farmersville Times*) and her husband began their interwoven newspaper careers ignorant of the entire publishing process.

The Linotype "took an instant dislike to me," she recalled. "I know it disliked me because it sprayed me with hot metal. It refused to distribute mats, or they fell flat, or they fell into the wrong channel and slowed my laborious task. But I learned."

By contrast, Mrs. C. K. Mick of the *Smithville Times* vowed she would "much rather operate the Linotype and do the thousand and one things connected with a newspaper than go back to the eternal dish washing, bed making, floor sweeping, etc." As the daughter of *Nixon News* publisher Frank Bridges, she had learned how to set type by hand as soon as she was big enough to sit in front of a type case. So the Linotype must have seemed as much of an advance to her as typesetting on computers did to a later generation.[8]

Consider the travails of the Compton family, who came to Mount En-terprise in 1919 to begin the new *Progress* with type packed in crates and boxes. On the train trip from Goliad, the type was jostled and jumbled out of order. Unscrambling the "pied type," as printers call it, was a routine task for Silas T. Compton's teenaged daughters—Zora, Vivian, and Rosalie. Integral to the family business, they also knew how to set type.[9]

As hemlines went up, so too rose women's fortunes in the newsroom. A group photograph made at the 1921 TPA convention in McAllen showed that women's fashions were changing from the Edwardian long dresses and large hats of the TPA's early conventions to a preview of the full "flapper" mode that characterized fashions of the 1920s.[10]

Less than ten years later, the fiftieth anniversary edition of the *Messenger* in 1929 contained individual photographs of four hundred TPA men and sixteen women.

Greater freedom in dress went along with greater opportunities for women to participate in the operations of weeklies and small dailies . As bookkeeping and financial management became more important, some publishers' wives found that niche most compatible.

John Esten Cooke of Rockdale, TPA president in 1921, referred to a new business model in his convention address, although there's no indication that he was specifically crediting women for the improved efficiencies. "The big outstanding feature is the increased evidence of better business methods put into practice by our members all over the state," Cooke said. "This . . . has been a long time coming."

Among the scores of publishers' wives who made notable but largely unseen contributions to their family business was Mrs. U. O. (Clemo) Clements of the *Panola Watchman* in Carthage. She stayed busy as bookkeeper, proofreader, office-supplies buyer and seller, and commercial-printing price estimator, just to name a few of her duties.

She described her husband as a writer of sometimes scathing editorials and a person who had "slap-happy views on economics." He paid no attention to monthly bills, she said, relying on her to make sure there was money in the bank.[11]

An earlier Carthage publisher, Miss Margie E. Neal of the *East Texas Register*, went on to become a state senator, and in that role campaigned successfully to make "Texas, Our Texas" the state song.

"Since giving up her newspaper at Carthage she has given more of her time to constructive work for the benefit of the people than any other citizen," the *Texas Press Messenger* reported in 1927.

Though women had already established themselves as indispensable "right hands," during World War II their roles in Texas newspapers both small and large expanded dramatically.

Lyde (Mrs. Charles) Devall was conscripted as publisher of the *Kilgore Daily News Herald* and weeklies in Daingerfield, Mount Vernon, and Hughes Springs during her husband's wartime navy service.

"Charlie and I got an awful kick out of a joke we heard while he was at home on leave," she said. "It seems a newspaperman came home one night and told his wife that he had joined the navy, and that she could run the paper while he went out to fight the Axis. She gave him one resigned look. Her only comment was: 'coward.'"

Introducing an article by Mrs. Devall, who had been asked to write on behalf of the wives of editors and publishers who had entered the armed forces, the January 1943 *Messenger* explained:

For years the work of such women as Mrs. Lee J. Roundtree of Bryan, Mrs. W. A. Salter of Kerrville, Mrs. Ross Woodall of Huntsville and Mrs. Seth Holman of Hereford has been outstanding in the publishing business. Frequently their attainments overshadowed the efforts of the so-called stronger sex. Now a new group of women are gaining distinction on Texas newspapers.

Eula Ann Kennedy achieved such distinction, confronting personal grief and the professional challenge of running a newspaper in wartime when her husband, J. A. Kennedy, died in 1943, only four months after he had purchased the *Chillicothe Valley News.*

An article in the 1954 *Messenger* reflected on her ensuing success. "When bids were made by prospects who hoped to obtain the newspaper for a song, Mrs. Kennedy—armed only with determination and faith in the newspaper, the town, and the fertile Chillicothe valley—made one of two decisions open to her. She rolled up her sleeves and went to work."

Plagued, like many other publishers, with labor and material shortages, she still managed to produce a column, "As Ann Sees It."[12]

Mrs. Arthur A. Sparkman, widowed in 1924, learned the newspaper business working as an employee in various jobs on the *Childress News and Index.* In 1939 she and her sons bought the *El Campo Citizen*, and during the war she and her son Warren operated with an all-woman staff.

But in the 1950s, articles in the *Texas Press Messenger* treated women of the TPA families as occupants of a separate sphere, regardless of their versatility in the workplace.

The seventy-fifth anniversary edition of the *Messenger*, published in 1954, segregated women publishers in a special section. Perhaps with ironic intent, the editor headed it with an 1893 quote from Mrs. Bishop about women being "perhaps not practical enough to meet the demands of modern newspapers."[13]

The special section profiled a dozen women, of whom only two, Corinne Neal Cook of the *Texas Mesquiter* in Mesquite and Wilma Amonette of the *Lone Oak News,* had gotten her newspaper by buying it.

Mrs. Cook, a world traveler, was a member of the Texas Independent Producers and Royalty Owners Association, perhaps a clue to her financial position.

Miss Amonette, however, became a publisher because she loved to operate the Linotype, a skill she learned at sixteen at the *Lone Oak News*. She was a full-time Linotypist for the *Greenville Herald Banner*, fourteen miles north of Lone Oak, when she bought the *News* from J. D. Rambo. She kept her day job at the *Banner*, bringing the type from Greenville and printing the paper herself on a small Diamond press.

Mrs. A. Cowan was among the profiled women publishers who married into the newspaper business. She assumed full control of the *San Saba Star* when her husband died, and in 1953, at age 79, she was still working. Accomplished at almost all the jobs from front office to back shop, she also wrote a column, "Jes Restin'," that was hardly descriptive of her life.[14]

Another publisher by marriage was Stella Gliddon, who took over the *Johnson City Record-Courier* when her husband died in 1940. Suddenly a single parent with six children, she found time to do her own yard work and to take part in church, club, and civic activities. Gliddon also served as Johnson City's postmaster, then a typical role for small town newspaper publishers. In 1935 the *Messenger* listed some thirty editor-postmasters.

But she was exceptional in that it was more often the male editor-publisher who also ran the post office. The 1954 *Messenger* reported that many a TPA member's wife sold advertising, printing, and subscriptions while the editor sold stamps.

The *Messenger*'s view of women as accessories gradually changed, as evidenced by a 1957 article acknowledging their unsung contributions. A story about the wives of thirteen TPA publishers carried the headline "It's a Woman's World."

The lead explained: "Such a short time ago it was taboo for a woman to work in public at all and now they make up an integral part of many professions. These stories indicate the extent of their help in making their husbands' newspapers successful, and the pride they take in a job well done."[15]

Two of the thirteen, Mrs. Joe T. Cook of the *Mission Times* and Mrs. Art Kowert of the *Fredericksburg Standard*, chose to do their newspaper work at home.

Elise Kowert said she kept her home phone line busy gathering news. She would make frequent trips to take her copy to the office and pick up notes for stories that had been sent in. Fortunately, the Kowerts lived only three blocks from the newspaper.

Mrs. Cook wrote her weekly column at home on the kitchen table. She said she seldom went to the office and went to conventions for purely social reasons: "to visit with friends, to compare and exhibit billfold pictures of the children, to wear my new hat to luncheons."

By contrast, Jerry Berger, copublisher of the *Hondo Anvil Herald* with her husband Bill, pointed out that convention "shop talk" was not exclusive to the men.

> We working women indulge in that too. And it has been the consensus of all with whom I have talked that we are playing an important part in helping our husbands get ahead and stay that way. With the weekly newspaper business, it is almost imperative that the husband and the wife consider it a vocation and an avocation—it's definitely love it or leave it.

Mrs. W. B. Crossley of the *Madisonville Meteor* said that she and her husband reversed the traditional roles of newspaper couples.

> I have observed that with other husband-wife teams, the wife sells the advertising and the husband stays in his office and writes news and editorials. But my husband sold advertising before he bought a newspaper of his own, and that is what he enjoys doing most. So, in the main, he handles the advertising and I the news. Although it is convenient that both of us can and will do anything that needs doing at the moment.

At the *New Braunfels Zeitung-Chronicle*, a typical day's work for Mrs. Frederic Oheim included trips to the post office, waiting on customers, writing stories, reading proof, folding a booklet, stuffing newspapers for mailing, taking ads over the phone, correcting the mailing list, and punching holes in notebook paper bought elsewhere.

Other days might bring just as many, but entirely different tasks, she said. What started as a part-time job had evolved into work that was "stimulating, if not immensely remunerative financially."

She learned not only the newspaper's stories but also "many of the facts that cannot be published." She said it would be hard to give up her work, which, among other advantages, had led to an understanding of her publisher-husband's problems and a source of interesting conversation with him.

In the *Messenger* story, Mrs. Lee A. Duewall of the *LaGrange Journal* spoke eloquently for the "ordinary housewife" pressed into service without prior training: "The publisher's wife fills more roles than mustard; she's wife, mother, cook and housemaid, chauffeur, nurse, veterinarian, garbage collector, and gardener in her spare time—and spare it is!"

And that's before she even gets to the office. Once there,

> She becomes all things to all people: bookkeeper, ad salesman, Miss Classified, circulation circumnavigator, printer's devil pro tem, proofreader,

band-aid dispenser to the backshop casualties, charwoman, sob sister, a Jane Arden girl reporter, defender of the faith, guardian of the truth, and possible pillar of strength to the publisher.

If she's lucky, she can also serve as Linotype operator, floor man, pressman, procurator of the mailbags and superintendent in charge of stamping and mailing. And through it all she moves, contented!

Mrs. Duewall observed that she has, in the last analysis, the greatest satisfaction of womankind—she gets the news first.[16]

Through the years a repeated theme, particularly among women involved with smaller family-newspaper operations, was the hardship involved in trying to get a break from the grind. Several mentioned that convention trips served this purpose, and so it was a natural evolution that the summer TPA convention became a traditional family vacation time.

Douglas and Helen Meador of the *Matador Tribune* said they received countless invitations they could not accept because the newspaper came first. For many years their weekend trips to press conventions were their only vacation.[17]

Mary Henkel Judson, who in 1990 became the first woman president of the Texas Press Association, grew up in just such a newspaper family. In the following essay she describes the road to journalism that took her from sidekick to publisher.

Family newspapers that have been passed down through the generations often involved spouses of the owners' sons and daughters. Sometimes the transitions were well planned, but other times the change was sudden, as in the case of Mrs. James R. Dennis of the *Jacksboro Gazette News*. This was her story:

For the first month after she was married in June 1950, she was a housewife who occasionally came down to the office where her husband shared the publisher's title with his mother.

Mrs. Dennis Sr. had become editor and publisher after her husband died in 1935. When James Jr. returned home from World War II in 1946, he became copublisher, but his mother kept the editor's job.

One Thursday afternoon when they had finished that week's paper, the elder Mrs. Dennis announced she was leaving the next day for an indefinite vacation that amounted to her retirement.

Overnight, the younger Mrs. Dennis, with two degrees in chemistry, became a newspaper partner, immersed in gathering news, keeping books, and selling advertising, among other duties.

"I feel I really earn my pay—50 cents per week for coffee money. An occasional thanks or compliment on the newspaper helps out," she reflected in the *Messenger* story.

But though the pay was short and the hours long, she said she couldn't think of another profession that was more challenging or satisfying.[19]

Versatility was the name of the game for the Dennis women and the many others like them who were born or married into (mostly smaller) community newspapers.

In Emory, "stand by your woman" represented role reversal at the *Rains County Leader*, where three generations of the large Hill family had published the paper since 1905. The third-generation publisher, Earl Clyde Hill Jr., left the newspaper in 1962, turning it over to his aunt, Kathleen Hill Becknell.

The *Messenger* reported in 1980 that she kept the *Leader* abreast of the times with "iron will and love."

"As she loves her community, it loves her. She enjoys and appreciates her husband, George Becknell, a capable writer [who covers local government] and who stands firmly by her in the day-to-day operation of the business."[18]

As weekly and small-daily newspapers converted to offset printing in the 1960s and '70s, many became attractive targets for acquisition by newspaper chains. The "50 cents for coffee" employee became a rarity, and the wife of a twenty-first-century male publisher is more likely to pursue her own career than help out as needed on the newspaper.

Women have steadily achieved status more nearly matching their contributions: in 2004, the Texas Press Association directory listed women publishers at 12 dailies and 105 weekly or semiweekly newspapers.

Martha Ann "Molly" Walls and her daughter Lissa Walls Vahldiek qualify as women newspaper executives because they own a newspaper company, Southern Newspapers Inc., although they aren't publishers in the strictest sense of the term. The family-owned organization adheres to a policy of editorial and managerial autonomy at their papers in Texas, Alabama, and Georgia.

For more than half a century, Molly Walls has symbolized the successful woman newspaper leader, from before she married the legendary newspaper leader B. Carmage Walls, side by side throughout their forty-four-year marriage and partnership that created newspaper holdings and companies across Texas and the southern United States, and today as she continues to actively manage a company that emphasizes community service in its newspapers.

Since 1967, when she became president and CEO of SNI, and following her husband's death in 1998, Walls has perpetuated the belief that newspapers should put more back into the communities they serve than they take out.

Lissa Walls Vahldiek, chief operating officer, follows the example her parents set for service to the newspaper industry. She serves on the board of directors of the Associated Press and has been president of the Texas Daily Newspaper Association.

Sue Mayborn is another trailblazing woman owner-publisher, overseeing operations at the *Temple Daily Telegram* and *Killeen Daily Herald*. In addition to the newspapers, the company also owns Channel 6 Inc., licensee of KCEN-TV, which serves the Waco-Temple-Killeen area.

Since 1987, she has been president of Frank Mayborn Enterprises Inc. She also serves on the AP board.

Perhaps Wanda Garner Cash, the 2004 Texas Press Association president, is emblematic of this change. Only the third woman to lead the TPA, she earned a journalism degree at the University of Texas at Austin in 1971, owned the *Ingram News* in rural Central Texas for eight years, and then moved into daily newspaper editing at the *Kerrville Daily Times*. Holding successively higher positions at three Gulf Coast dailies, she is now publisher of the daily *Baytown Sun*.

In an interview for this essay, Cash recalled balancing her days as a weekly publisher, part-time high school journalism teacher, and mother:

> Our sons literally grew up at the office. When our youngest was born in 1982, it was a Tuesday, deadline day. I took the rest of the week off and was back on Monday with the baby in a big basket next to my desk. I didn't regard it as heroic or unusual. I believe a community newspaper is like a public utility and we had a paper to get out.

In 1893 the Austin journalist and literary critic, Bride Neill Taylor, wrote a two-part series in the *Galveston News* on women writers of Texas. Speaking on their behalf, she concluded, "she has a dignified view of woman's field in literature and journalism and thinks they ought to be paid the full value of their services—not so much, she says, for the sake of the pay as for the injustice of working for nothing."[20]

That injustice has largely been corrected today, Mrs. Taylor might be pleased to know.

SARAH LASCHINGER GREENE *is copublisher with her son, William R. Greene, of the* Gilmer Mirror. *She represents the third generation to manage the family-owned semiweekly newspaper, which was founded in 1877 and was purchased by her grandfather, George Tucker, in 1915. After receiving a bachelor of journalism degree from the University of Texas at Austin in 1949, she worked for three years as a reporter for the* Dallas Morning News.

She has served as president of the Texas Press Association, from which she received the Golden 50 Award, and the North and East Texas Press Association, which presented her the Sam C. Holloway Memorial Award. She has been president of the Texas Folklore Society and a director of the East Texas Historical Association, and has written essays and book reviews for their publications, among others.

NOTES

1. *Texas Press Messenger*, June 1957, 12.
2. *Texas Press Messenger*, Golden Anniversary edition, 1929.
3. Proceedings of the 10th annual Texas Press Association convention, El Paso, May 1889, 45–46.
4. *History of the Texas Press*, F. B. Baillio, 1916.
5. Sylvia Ann Grider and Lou Halsell Rodenberger, *Texas Women Writers* (College Station: Texas A&M Univ. Press, 1997), 5.
6. *Texas Press Messenger*, Golden Anniversary edition, 1929.
7. *Texas Press Messenger*, 75th anniversary edition, June 1954, 79.
8. *Texas Press Messenger*, June 1957, 10–11.
9. *Texas Press Messenger*, 100th anniversary edition, June 1980, 235.
10. Photograph hanging in Texas Press Association headquarters, Austin.
11. *Texas Press Messenger*, June 1957, 15–16.
12. *Texas Press Messenger*, June 1954, 101.
13. Ibid., 97.
14. Ibid., 97–101.
15. *Texas Press Messenger*, June 1957, 10.
16. Ibid., 10–16.
17. *Texas Press Messenger*, June 1980, 160.
18. Ibid., 133.
19. *Texas Press Messenger*, June 1957, 14–15.
20. Grider and Rodenberger, *Texas Women Writers*, 64.

CHAPTER 9

On the Fast Track

WOMEN MAKE STRIDES AS DAILIES RECORD
A 44 PERCENT INCREASE IN THE NUMBER OF FEMALE PUBLISHERS

PAULINE WORD

A new face is emerging in Texas's newspaper management, and she is making history in her climb to the top. Women are steadily gaining ground into the publisher's seat, and they're bringing the industry into a new era.

Men traditionally have held newspaper management, but women publishers now serve at 24 percent of Texas newspapers. The most recent and dramatic change is among daily newspapers: Texas's 90 dailies experienced a 44 percent increase in the number of women publishers from May 2003 to March 2004. And since September 2003 two dailies—each more than 100 years old—entered historic territory by hiring their first-ever female publishers.

Women have long been trailblazers at Texas weeklies, where 27 percent of publishers are women, many of whom own and operate their own newspapers. But women in management at semiweeklies and dailies lag behind their male counterparts: only thirteen of ninety dailies, nine of fifty-eight semiweeklies, and two triweeklies have women publishers.

For the first time in TPA's 125-year history, the association is poised to elect back-to-back women presidents and the first-ever woman from a daily newspaper—Wanda Garner Cash, editor and publisher of the *Baytown Sun*—took office in June 2004. Judy Johnson, publisher of the *Hometown Press* in Winnie, is in line for the top spot in June 2005.

Cash, who has been in her present position since August 1999, was pleased with the growing number of women publishers at Texas dailies. "I'm encouraged to see women making those strides," she said.

The new women publishers all are at small—less than 10,000 in circulation—Texas dailies.

"I think it's a cultural and a generational change. Plus, men are more accepting of women in management and leadership roles today," Cash said.

Two other women have served as TPA president: the first in 1990–1991,

Mary Judson, copublisher of the weekly *Port Aransas South Jetty*, and in 1995–1996 Sarah Greene, publisher of the semiweekly *Gilmer Mirror*.

"Those shoes are bigger than mine, and I'm going to have a hard time filling them," Cash said of her female predecessors.

TIMES ARE A-CHANGING

In January 2004 Amy Miller was named the first woman publisher of the 100-year-old *Jacksonville Daily Progress*, which is owned by Community Newspaper Holdings Inc. (CNHI). The preceding September, Karla DeLuca became the first woman to lead the 105-year-old *Nacogdoches Daily Sentinel.*

Miller took the reins in Jacksonville after coming up through the advertising side of the business and serving as advertising director for a year and a half. She joined the *Progress* staff in June 2002 and is excited about her first job as publisher. "I love it," Miller said. "I'm learning a lot. It's a challenge."

Miller said she learned from the previous publisher, Bill Morgan, who moved to sister newspaper, the *Athens Daily Review*, that "making each department work together" is the key to publishing a great newspaper. "I think the key is the team that you have," she said.

Women publishers face different challenges from men in the same role and may meet resistance to change from their communities and even from staff members. But all the new female publishers seem ready for the challenge.

In Nacogdoches, DeLuca welcomes being a test case as the *Sentinel*'s first female publisher; she also is the editor, and comes from the editorial side. She came from another Cox-owned newspaper, the *Marshall News Messenger*, where she had been managing editor since 1999.

"This is different because you get to deal with all the aspects of the newspaper," she said. "I really enjoy learning new things."

DeLuca replaced Gary Borders, who moved to another sister newspaper, the *Lufkin Daily News.*

In Orange, Charlotte Lynch became only the second woman publisher of the 129-year-old newspaper. The position had been vacant until 2004, when Glenn Stifflemire stepped in as regional publisher in Orange and publisher of sister CNHI property, the *Port Arthur News*. He hired Lynch to take over at the *Leader.*

"I'm ecstatic," Lynch said. "My community here is absolutely fabulous. It's been a wonderful transition to finally accept a publisher position."

Lynch has been in newspapers since the '90s, and came up on the advertising side, working for CNHI papers in Oklahoma and serving as the company's regional advertising director in Iowa.

"I was proud to be chosen for this position," she said of the publisher role. "I'm still smiling after so many years of hard work. . . . I love this business."

In 2001 Judy Allen became the first female publisher of the 78-year-old *Borger News-Herald*. Allen has been at the newspaper off and on since 1974, and rose through the ranks after starting as a runner for advertising proofs and tear sheets.

"I love this newspaper," said Allen, who sees no difference between male and female publishers. The key, she said, is developing a good rapport with customers to gain their respect.

"It's a very rewarding job. It's busy and it's hectic," she said.

Eight other women serve in the top post at Texas dailies: thirteen dailies have women publishers, but Sue Mayborn is publisher of both the *Temple Daily Telegram* and *Killeen Daily Herald*, so in all twelve women hold publisher jobs.

Susanne Reed took over at the *Big Spring Herald* in January 2004, replacing interim publisher Chuck Williams. Brenda Adams became publisher at the *Sweetwater Reporter* in the summer of 2003.

Longtime daily women publishers include Pearl Austin Mathis of the *Edinburg Daily Review* and the weekly *Rio Grande Herald*; Genevieve Ratcliff, editor and publisher of the *Fort Worth Commercial Recorder*; Helen Lutz at the *San Antonio Commercial Recorder*; Lynette Copley at the *Mexia Daily News*; as well as Cash and Mayborn.

Additionally, two women serve as copublishers of Texas dailies: Susan Clay at the *Dalhart Daily Texan* and Linda Shepard at the *Coastal Bend Legal and Business News* in Corpus Christi.

WOMEN IN THE NATION

In 2003 the Media Management Center at Northwestern University completed a three-year study of women in newspaper management. The final report "Women in Newspapers 2003: Challenging the Status Quo" was written by Mary Arnold and Marlene Lozada Hendrickson.

The report found that the nation's 137 largest newspapers (circulation more than 85,000) are led by 25 women and 112 men. The report showed that the percentage of publishers, presidents, and CEOs who were women increased from 14 percent in 2002 to 18 percent in 2003, even though the overall number of women in daily-newspaper management remains low.

The percentage of women executives remains the highest in personnel, marketing, and community affairs, according to the study, but those areas are not on the preferred track for moving into the highest positions. In editorial departments, 40 percent of managing editors are women, but only 22 percent of those at the top of the news department are women.

Overall, women comprise 46 percent of the U.S. workforce, but head up just 8 percent of the Fortune 500 companies. The same is true in at the highest levels of government. Women occupy only 8 of the 50 governor's mansions and 61 of the 435 seats in the U.S. House of Representatives. There are 14 female U.S. senators and 3 women among the 14 cabinet members.

WEEKLY WOMEN

At Texas weekly newspapers, the picture is brighter: 27 percent of the 377 publishers are women. Eight women also own and publish multiple weekly newspapers, and some Texas weeklies have an all-women staff. And in Texas newspaper groups, several women also serve as publisher of two weekly newspapers.

Gilmer publisher Sarah Greene was pleased to learn of the increase in women daily publishers, especially within group-owned newspapers. "That just shows there are opportunities for capable women to move on up," Greene said.

Historically, independent newspapers are run by a husband and wife, the woman serving as editor or advertising director and the man as publisher, Greene said. Leadership of many of those newspapers passes to the woman with the death of a spouse or parent.

Greene also attributed the increase in the number of women in newspaper management to more women choosing it as a career. "I think there are more women in journalism now," she said.

(This article appeared in substantially the same form in the *Texas Press Messenger*, March 2004)

PAULINE WORD *is publications manager for the Texas Press Association, where she edits the* Texas Press Messenger *and the* TPA Bulletin *and coordinates editorial content for www.texaspress.com. Word received a bachelor of arts in journalism from the University of Houston in May 1991.*

She has been a reporter at the Clear Lake Citizen *(then a daily), editor of the weekly* Cleveland Advocate, *and reporter and assistant news editor at the daily* Conroe Courier. *She also did a stint as editor of two "This Week" sections at the* Houston Chronicle, *and was editor of two monthly home-and-living magazines in Austin before joining TPA in 1998.*

CHAPTER 10

The Wire

MIKE COCHRAN

EDITOR'S NOTE: *When the Associated Press celebrated its 150th anniversary in 1998, Fort Worth correspondent Mike Cochran, whose AP career spanned the final four decades of the twentieth century, took a lighthearted look at the history of the international news service in Texas. His account has been updated and slightly revised for this anthology.*

"A dark abode of barbarism and vice," grumbled H. S. Foote.
"A valley of rascals," complained a Whig campaign paper.
"An Elysium of rogues," sniffed Kentuckian James Pettie.
"A den of thieves," snorted newspaper publisher Horace Greeley.
Those pithy observations come from folks carping about Texas and Texans in general, and were collected by Jerry Flemmons in his book *Texas Siftings*. But the history of Texas and the Texas Associated Press go pretty much hand in hand, if one can bend or suspend belief a mite here and there. And for this there is justification, as set forth by the late Dallas columnist Paul Crume. "Outsiders never understand that Texas tall talk is not a lie," said he. "It is the expression of the larger truth."
So with all the fanfare surrounding the AP's 150th anniversary, it seemed not only appropriate but also obligatory that we in Texas look back on our role in this historical milestone. It is no great stretch to say that Texas newspapers and the Texas AP grew up together, linked first by Morse operators and today by satellites in space.
It was on or about May 14, 1848, that representatives of six New York City newspapers met to form the Associated Press. Today, the AP is the world's oldest and largest news-gathering organization. Serving more than 17,000 newspaper, radio, and television outlets in 121 nations, the AP is a window on the world for millions of people.

Back in 1848, the AP was created simply to save money, a scheme to reduce costs by pooling resources to collect international news from incoming ships. Now the not-for-profit news cooperative produces about 20 million words, a thousand photographs, worldwide video feeds, and hundreds of voice reports each day.

The AP has more than 240 bureaus around the world, providing such a broad scope that Mark Twain once observed: "There are only two forces that can carry light to all corners of the globe—only two—the sun in the heavens and the Associated Press down here."

Details are a bit vague on just how, when, and where the news service began in the Lone Star State, but according to an AP historian, the first verifiable AP man in Texas was John P. Boughan, who came here in 1884. Boughan was stationed at Galveston as "agent" for the old Western Associated Press. He remained in Texas for a year, and then went to Chicago to work principally as a markets editor until his retirement fifty-four years later.

From its early, humble, and sketchy beginnings, the AP in Texas grew to 100 newspaper members, more than any other domestic AP territory.

The Texas AP also serves roughly 200 radio and television stations, providing material not only for broadcasts but for Web sites as well. The far-flung operation has seventy writers, editors, photographers, technicians, and others stationed in Dallas and seven satellite bureaus: Houston, Austin, San Antonio, Fort Worth, El Paso, Lubbock, and the Rio Grande Valley.

There's even an embassy of sorts in Washington, D.C., although corporate types call it a regional writer position. Texas newspapers and broadcasters share their local news and photos, making AP a historically unique concept in newsgathering.

Since the news headquarters opened in Dallas on January 11, 1911, there have been fourteen Texas bureau chiefs. Five are still living: Bob Johnson, Jim Mangan, Dorman Cordell, John Lumpkin, and the current chief of bureau, Dale Leach. Lumpkin remains in Texas as the first-ever AP regional vice president overseeing eleven states, including Texas.

It was Johnson, the chief executive from 1962 until 1969, who wrote the Texas AP's most famous bulletin:

DALLAS, NOV. 22 (AP)—PRESIDENT KENNEDY WAS SHOT TODAY JUST AS HIS MOTORCADE LEFT DOWNTOWN DALLAS. MRS. KENNEDY JUMPED UP AND GRABBED MR. KENNEDY. SHE CRIED, "OH, NO!" THE MOTORCADE SPED ON.

Mangan, the assistant bureau chief who would succeed Johnson six years

Jack Ruby shoots Lee Harvey Oswald—November 23, 1963—in the basement of the Dallas Police Station. *Photo © Bob Jackson. Used courtesy of the photographer.*

later, was also present that incredible day in 1963. Mangan's legacy also includes a searing piece that sheds new light on the "Box 13" election scandal that propelled Lyndon Johnson into the U.S. Senate.

And it was Mangan who, by circumstance, helped launch the national career of a feisty young woman named Linda.

Linda surfaced in Dallas about the same time as those early, crude, and still-mysterious computers. Late one night, while working the broadcast desk, she composed a letter on her new electronic wonder. Intended for a male friend, the message was vaguely intimate and also contained an unflattering reference to her new boss.

Linda ended the missive with words to the effect that, if she were to push the wrong button, AP members in three states would be reading her epic the next morning with their Post Toasties.

Needless to say, Linda proceeded to push the no-no button.

Mangan was alerted by telephone at daybreak, and Linda's ties to the AP ended abruptly. As luck would have it, a Houston television station, mightily impressed with Linda's writing ability—so eloquently demonstrated in her letter—offered her a job. From Houston she moved to New York and on to quirky prominence as network TV journalist Linda Ellerbee.

Brief though it was, Ms. Ellerbee's AP career was no match for that of an AP staffer we nicknamed the "one-day correspondent." Dispatched to his new post in San Antonio, the young man proceeded to introduce himself by offering to buy a newspaper colleague a drink.

Unnecessary, his new friend replied. Our man insisted. The colleague declined. Nasty words were exchanged. So our guy slugged him, which amused neither the San Antonio membership nor the Texas AP bureau chief. And the next day our hero was history.

Texas and its AP staff have never suffered from a shortage of major news stories, dating back to the post-Boughan era, when the operation was largely in the hands of the AP Morse operators.

"They were the frontiersmen for the AP, spreading out over the state as new members joined and telegraph lines were extended," AP historian Raymond Holbrook reported.

He noted that 1910 was a pivotal year for the Texas AP, marked by the arrival of Memphis correspondent T. C. Ashcroft. "When he finished his tour he had lined up 100 stringers over the state, had started a new wire for day service, and had set the stage for the Dallas bureau," Holbrook wrote.

An AP service bulletin of 1911 modestly reported that Texas newspaper members were "positively thrilled" at having their own state wire. The first demands of the seven morning papers: stories and boxes on all the Texas League baseball games.

Probably the biggest breaking story in the early days of the Dallas bureau involved the activities of Pancho Villa and his revolutionists across the border in Mexico. In one memorable episode, bureau chief Howard Blakeslee was about to cross the Rio Grande on a dubious and perilous mission when his Mexican guide began waving an American flag.

"That made us as conspicuous as a horse on Broadway," Blakeslee said later. "All at once, wham! And the bullets began to fly."

Blakeslee survived, got his story, and when the United States took action, covered General John J. Pershing's expedition into Mexico. He would later become AP's first science writer.

Through the years, the Texas AP has covered too many national blockbusters to list, but few twentieth-century disaster stories rival the New London school explosion on March 18, 1937. It killed 294 people, most of them children. Old-timers still insist that news coverage of the tragedy would become a model of AP staff effort and member cooperation.

I came along in the early 1960s, just in time for the assassination of President Kennedy and the subsequent slaying of Lee Harvey Oswald. After

Jack Ruby murdered Oswald, I became a historical footnote of sorts. Nobody showed up to carry Oswald's casket at Fort Worth's Rose Hill Cemetery, so reporters were recruited as pallbearers. I was one of them.

Some would conclude later that the assassination coverage was the finest moment of the AP in Texas. But the essence of the story was spotlighted this way, in a message to the entire staff from the late general manager Wes Gallagher: "The point to take pride in is that we were participants in one of the critical and emotional moments in the history of man and reported it fully and objectively, accurately and clearly in good taste."

I remembered Gallagher's "emotional moments" comment six years later on yet another story. It was at the Johnson Space Center when Neil Armstrong climbed from his Apollo 11 spacecraft *Eagle* and planted a footprint on the moon.

Not unlike other states, Texas staffers have covered floods, hurricanes, tornadoes, droughts, plane crashes, politics, and scandals. But few states have coped with the likes of University of Texas Tower sniper Charles Whitman, flimflam artist Billie Sol Estes, would-be presidential assassin John Hinckley, serial rapist-killers Kenneth McDuff and Henry Lee Lucas, Depression-era bandit couple Bonnie and Clyde, and a renowned Methodist minister named Walker Railey, who was accused but not convicted of trying to kill his wife so he could marry his striking mistress. And long before O. J. there was Cullen Davis, a Fort Worth zillionaire whose 1977 murder trial was then the longest and costliest in the nation's history. He, too, was acquitted.

Then there was the defining story of the Texas nineties. We had hardly heard of David Koresh until February 28, 1993. Yet AP staffers would stand on a road near his Branch Davidian compound or work out of a makeshift office on the ground floor of the Holiday Inn in Waco for the next fifty-one days. More than a decade later, the image of the inferno is seared in our memories.

The late Bob Ford, a beloved grump and a tough and demanding AP state editor, insisted that Texas staffers must know, or soon learn, about a number of things. In part, they included timber, oil, cattle, steel, coal, electronics, satellite speeds, exotic dancers, and Jayne Mansfield's private Dallas phone number. Also football rankings, major league batting averages, Juarez divorce laws, underworld heroin prices, soil erosion, and the smell of marijuana.

Also, the dangerous quadrant of a hurricane, the paths tornadoes take, urban renewal, water conservation, cow prices, freeze damage point, and John Birch. He also mentioned space, even before the NASA facility in Texas began controlling the missions that took men to the moon and back beginning in the late 1960s.

Ford was also around for the building of the Astrodome in Houston, the national championships of Darrell Royal's Texas Longhorns, and the rise of the Dallas Cowboys under Tom Landry. But he would miss the boom and bust of Jerry Jones's Cowboys under spray-haired Jimmy Johnson and gun-toting Barry Switzer, as well as the college football payola scandal that reached the Texas governor's office.

Bizarre, Byzantine, or just colorfully weird politicians are hardly unique to Texas, but not many other AP bureaus have dealt so consistently with political figures such as presidents Lyndon Johnson and George Bush the elder; governors Pappy Lee O'Daniel, Pa and Ma Ferguson, John Connally, and Ann Richards; billionaire wild-card presidential candidate Ross Perot; and longtime U.S. House Speaker Sam Rayburn. We don't claim Bill Clinton, but Paula Jones was represented by a Dallas law firm. And who could have envisioned that a former Texas governor, George W. Bush, would guide America through the trauma of 9/11 and into a war with Iraq in 2003?

And through it all, the hallmark of the Texas AP has been its special spirit of cooperation with its members. Time and again I worked hand in glove with newspaper and broadcast staffers all across the state.

After devastating tornadoes in Lubbock and Wichita Falls about a decade apart, the AP literally set up shop in the newsrooms of the *Lubbock Avalanche-Journal* and the *Wichita Falls Times and Record-News*.

Through the cooperative efforts of the *Pecos News, El Paso Times, Abilene Reporter-News, Big Spring Herald*, and others, including the weekly *Brady Standard*, we rode shotgun on the adventures of con artist Billie Sol Estes for more than forty years.

The *Sweetwater Reporter* was the inspiration for one of the most successful series to appear on the AP wire: a murder case christened "Prairie Justice."

The *Lufkin News* shared an investigative story with us and won a Pulitzer Prize.

I was in the Dallas bureau after Jack Ruby gunned down Lee Harvey Oswald, and was privy early on to Bob Jackson's stunning photograph that the *Dallas Times Herald* offered to the AP. Of course, it, too, won a Pulitzer.

More recently, the *Tyler Morning Telegraph* contacted the AP after viewing the images of the shuttle *Columbia* breaking up over Texas on the morning of February 1, 2003. The AP purchased the rights to the photos from Tyler cardiologist Scott Lieberman and distributed the images around the world. In 2004, the news service submitted the images for Pulitzer consideration in spot news photography.

"It was the single widest-used image to illustrate a breaking news event of all time," Bob Daugherty, director of the AP State Photo Center in Washington, D.C., reported.

Indeed, we may be, as those critics maintain, rascals, rogues, thieves, barbaric, and too quick to stretch the truth. But as Bob Ford pointed out more than forty years ago: "It's pretty hard to be bored in Texas."

After early stints at the Denton Record Chronicle *and the* Abilene Reporter-News, **MIKE COCHRAN** *spent thirty-nine years roving Texas, mostly West Texas, for the Associated Press. Based much of that time in Fort Worth, he joined the* Star-Telegram *in 1999 as a senior writer. He retired in 2003, and is currently working on his fourth and fifth books: authorized biographies of West Texas rancher-wildcatter-politico Clayton Williams Jr. and Las Vegas poker legend Doyle "Texas Dolly" Brunson.*

CHAPTER 11

The Role of Humor Writing in Texas Newspapers

JACK LOFTIS

It's fortunate that God did not include "Thou Shalt Be Funny" as the Eleventh Commandment. If he had, the world's sinners probably would have already overtaken the righteous, and Hell would be an endless string of amateur nights at a second-rate comedy club.

Humor is a tough game in any realm. But to achieve it successfully in a newspaper, and on a regular schedule, is as difficult as it gets. Most self-respecting newspaper reporters and columnists would never admit they were trying to write humorously. It just isn't done, because the risk of failure is too high. Those who are willing to give humor a shot would prefer to be identified as general-topic columnists and feature writers. Then, if the laughs come . . . well, it just happened.

Accidentally, intentionally, or whatever, humorous prose has always been an essential element of most newspapers. Today it is perhaps the best defense available to counter the totally incorrect charge that newspapers are only interested in gloom and doom "because they help sell papers."

To the contrary, when the *Houston Post* shuttered its doors in 1995, columnists Mickey Herskowitz and Ken Hoffman, two fine writers who know how to tease and entertain readers, were among the first hires by the surviving *Houston Chronicle*. Media bashers will be annoyed to learn that the failed newspaper's obituary writers and crime reporters were placed on *Chronicle* waiting lists.

Had he just chosen one keyboard over another, classical pianist Victor Borge would have made a splendid funnyman in print. He had it right when he said: "Humor is something that thrives between man's aspirations and his limitations. There is more logic in humor than in anything else. Because, you see, humor is truth."

True or false, Lynn Ashby, a former *Houston Post* columnist and the editor of the newspaper's editorial page, believes nothing is worse than someone who is not funny trying to be funny. Ashby discovered he had a knack for humor while attending the University of Texas as a pre-med student in the 1960s.

"I went to work on the campus humor magazine, the *Texas Ranger,* and readers laughed at my stories," Ashby said. "I found that enormously satisfying, more so than cutting up frogs. So I switched my major to journalism."

Austin American-Statesman columnist John Kelso believes the key to successfully writing humorous prose is to first become a good reporter. "Find out what people in town are talking about, then put a funny twist on it," he said. "For example, a few years ago UT regents didn't like the proposed design of their new Blanton Art Museum. It was done by a European architectural firm, and it was modernistic and somewhat 'Jetsons' in appearance. The regents said they wanted a design that would be familiar to all Texans, and that being the case, I suggested they find an architect to design a museum that looked like a Dairy Queen."

Columnist and author Leon Hale, whose often-humorous work has appeared in the *Houston Chronicle* and the *Houston Post* for more than fifty years, enjoys writing about his growing up in small Texas towns and his continuing efforts to cope with life in the big city.

"I'm not sure if I have a philosophy about writing fun stuff," Hale said. "But I decided long ago that when I read, what I want more than anything else is to be entertained. Even when I'm reading to get information of the deepest importance to me, I retain that information best when it's presented in a light and entertaining style. So, that's how I try to write." And with great success, one must add.

A *Chronicle* reader once said that reading Hale "makes me laugh as if I were hearing him tell a story while the two of us were sitting on the front porch of his old country house near Winedale." But Hale says he never thinks about making his readers laugh out loud. "That's for comedy writers, and it's terribly difficult to do consistently," he said. "I'd rather get a hint of a grin at the corner of his mouth, or a smile in his eye, that stays there all the way to the end of the piece—and a while afterward."

The history of Texas newspapers is rich with the wit and wisdom of such writers as Hale. Our minds easily drift back to the stereotyped image of the country editor that Hollywood has served up in endless Westerns. You remember him: about sixty, gray beard, eyeshade, and dark sleeve protectors. He seldom wrote at his desk, but barked out stories to a shy apprentice who would immediately convert the words into type. Mark Twain undoubtedly was the inspiration for the earliest Texas publishers and editors who were willing to view events around them through a twinkling eye. Later motivation was provided by Oklahoma native Will Rogers, whose syndicated newspaper column was published throughout the Lone Star State.

Writing in the *Texas Press Messenger* in June 1954 to celebrate the Texas Press Association's seventy-fifth anniversary, University of Texas journalism professor Olin Hinkle pointed out that "the life of the small-town editors is being revealed week by week in home grown columns of wit, humor, pathos, sentiment, anecdotes, exhortations, apologies and other items ranging from profoundest editorial opinion to just plain trivia."

The humor—as it was—came in short takes, usually local and personal and always insightful. Hinkle described the writing as "truisms of quick impact."

"Jim Jones blames his being late for church Sunday on a milk cow that broke out of her pen. Just goes to prove that the trouble with milk cows is they won't stay milked."

"My wife says I am in trouble if I write that teachers, bankers, and hoot owls sleep with one eye open."

"Banker Thompson says he warns his customers that mortgaging a crop is like saddling a wobbly colt. You may not make it."

The writing was not bad, considering such gems preceded the late-night humor of Johnny Carson, Jay Leno, and David Letterman. A grossly limited list of editors and publishers who understood that humor was vital to the success of their newspapers—and whose careers were linked by the Texas Press Association—included H. H. "Buttermilk" Lowry of Honey Grove, Russell Bryant of Italy, Clint Thompson of McKinney, O. C. Harrison of Seymour, H. M. Baggarly of Tulia, Archer Fullingim of Kountze, Wick Fowler of Austin, H. B. Fox of Taylor, and an early TPA president, Uncle Dan McGary of Brenham.

Even the names of several Texas newspapers promote smiles: the *Ferris Wheel, Omaha Breeze, Port Lavaca Wave, Big Lake Wildcat, Cedar Hill Merry-Go-Round,* and everyone's all-time favorite, the *Jefferson Jimplecute.* Legend has it that the editor was trying to come up with a name for his paper when he dropped a box of type on the floor. The result: J I M P L E C U T E.

The writing of Fox, who was publisher of the weekly *Taylor Times,* carried enough humorous punch to gain syndication, and was featured in many of his peers' newspapers. A good example of his style is this observation following a trip to New York City:

And the Empire State Building with its 120 stories is just a monotonous repetition of a two-story building we've had down here in Williamson County for years. In proportion to population Circleville has as many neon lights as Broadway, and they attract as many moths.

ACE REID: A RESONANCE THAT STILL RINGS TRUE
WANDA GARNER CASH

Jake and Zeb, the hardscrabble cowboys from the Draggin' S Ranch, are emblematic of born-in-Texas cartoon humor.

Ace Reid, acknowledged dean of cowboy cartoonists and member of the Cowboy Hall of Fame, created the one-panel *Cowpokes* series, modeling the iconic characters after his own experiences in Depression-era Texas.

Reid grew up shocking wheat, breaking horses, and fixing fences on his father's 4,000-acre ranch in Electra, Texas. But with his natural ability for art, Reid decided early on that it was easier to draw cowboys than to be one. He studied fine art at the Abbott School in Washington, D.C., but it was Reid's cartooning that made him famous and made Jake and Zeb beloved across America.

He sold his first cartoon in 1949, to the *Quarterhorse Journal* for $3. Reid's widow Madge recalled that he drove 150 miles "there and back" to deliver the cartoon.

Reid drew the beloved *Cowpokes* series until he died in 1991. Today, Madge Reid perpetuates the Draggin' S legacy, selling *Cowpokes* books, prints, and calendars and syndicating the cartoons.

"I'll be glad to let my pastures rest for a couple of years if you'll get my banker and the tax collector to let me rest the same length of time."

"Ace left me a lot of cartoons," she said. "He told me if I'd take care of the business right, nobody would know he was gone. A lot of papers didn't print his obituary."

At the height of the cartoon's popularity, it was running in 500 newspapers, thanks to early assistance from Ace and Madge's friend, Houston Harte, cofounder of Harte-Hanks Communications, who was publisher in San Angelo when they first knew him.

The original success came from big daily papers in Fort Worth, Houston, San Antonio, and, of course, San Angelo, when Texas was still considered a rural state and agricultural coverage was a significant news beat.

Jake and Zeb's earthy pontifications resonated with the farm-and-ranch crowd, who recognized the authentic characters and plot lines in Reid's cartoons.

As the metro papers reduced their coverage of crops and livestock, *Cowpokes* moved into the weekly markets and beyond Texas. From their home in Kerrville, Ace was the artist and Madge ran the business.

"But Ace did all the selling," Madge said. "We never missed a Texas Press convention, knew all the publishers by name."

Cowpokes appears in about 250 newspapers these days, continuing its wry observations cloaked in worn jeans and dusty boots. The cattle are still skinny, and Jake and Zeb equally underfed, but the universal theme of striving fills a nation's need to laugh at ourselves as we plug along.

WANDA GARNER CASH is editor and publisher of the *Baytown Sun*. She was the 125th president of the Texas Press Association.

But the Texas journalist whose versatility set the bar for laughter was Morris Frank, columnist, toastmaster, radio-television commentator, and the best public-relations representative the *Houston Chronicle* has ever known. Frank, who died in 1975, also served as sports editor of the *Houston Post* before moving to the *Chronicle*, where he reached his full potential while writing his popular "Cabbages and Kings" column. Frank was born in Lufkin and worked in his father's clothing store while also writing sports for the *Lufkin Daily News* and serving as a correspondent for the *Post*.

Realizing that it had discovered a diamond in the rough, the *Post* offered Frank full-time employment in Houston. "I don't know if a journalist was born that day, but I damn sure know a dry-goods salesman died," Frank would often say. As an extension of his fame as a writer, Frank was much in demand as a toastmaster, appearing at major events throughout the nation. His trademark was barbed, yet not mean-spirited, observations about almost everyone in the audience—especially himself.

University of Houston journalism professor David McHam remembers seeing Frank at his best at one of Houston restaurateur Bill Williams's famed Capon Dinners in the 1950s. The stag event was so popular that it was held in a circus tent, and on this particular night a thunderstorm was drenching the area.

McHam said that halfway through the evening, a fight broke out between Glenn McCarthy, the notorious wildcatter–hotel owner, and another guest. As they struggled, they dislodged a tent pole, and rainwater began to pour inside. McHam said that Frank saw what was happening, turned to the orchestra, and said, "It's time for 'The Star-Spangled Banner.'" The anthem was played, everyone stood at attention, and Frank again had taken control of the night.

Austin's Cactus Pryor could almost match Frank's dual talents, writing a humor column that was widely syndicated while also being in demand as a toastmaster and speaker. He would often begin his talks using affected accents and clever disguises, then would reveal his identity as his audience sat spellbound, often in shock.

The comical Wick Fowler of Austin once published a political weekly called the *Town Crier*. A talented pundit who later would become the executive assistant to Texas governor Allan Shivers, Fowler's real fame would occur on the chili-cook-off circuit, and his own products today sit on the shelves of groceries across the nation.

Women certainly have had a major role in conveying laughter through the pages of Texas newspapers. One who is quite adept is Liz Carpenter of Austin. Her writing career began at the *Daily Texan* on the University of Texas campus and

Correspondents Les and Liz Carpenter. *From the Prints and Photographs Collection, Center for American History, The University of Texas at Austin.*

continued at the *Austin American-Statesman* prior to her going to Washington as press secretary for Lady Bird Johnson during the LBJ White House years.

Since returning to Austin to resume her career as a writer and speaker, Carpenter has authored four books, including her best-selling *Start with a Laugh*, and has contributed freelance articles to newspapers and magazines all over Texas.

"I grew up in a family of talkers at dinnertime, and because it was the Depression, you had to laugh," Carpenter said. " My mother was a scholar and had a great wit, and that made all the difference. You listen for humor. You read humor. You steal humor. You reuse humor."

One of Carpenter's best stories is credited to former U.S. congressman Jake Pickle of Austin. Briefly—and Carpenter insists that timing while speaking and not wasting words when writing are keys to being humorous—while President Johnson was reading a speech prepared for him, he spotted a quote from Socrates in the text. "These folks have never heard of Socrates," he said while reaching for a pen. "Let's make it read, 'As my dear old father used to say . . .'"

Carpenter credits the late Erma Bombeck, whose humor column was syndicated in more than a thousand newspapers, as her major inspiration. "I learned a lot from Erma firsthand when we traveled weekends for the Equal Rights Amendment," she recalls. "We talked often on the phone and exchanged jokes. Her sources of humor were generally family things, which made her the No. 1 clipboard on refrigerators. I really miss her."

There is no doubt that Bombeck influenced many other Texas writers. In 1956 June Benefield began writing "Skirt Tales" for the *Houston Chronicle* in a very Bombeckian style. Years later *Chronicle* readers were treated to more laughs by Linda Griffin, while Marilyn Schwartz of the *Dallas Morning News* and Bonnie Gangelhoff of the *Houston Post* were producing somewhat similar styles of humor. Unfortunately, health problems ended Schwartz's career at the *News*, the closing of the *Post* silenced Gangelhoff, and a bad decision by *Chronicle* editors converted Griffin into a full-time fashion writer, thus suppressing a talent that might have blossomed nationally.

Much of the humor presented in the newspapers of Texas over the years has had its roots in politics—and satirical, often cruel, points of view have been its trademarks.

Years ago C. L. Douglas, the associate editor of the old *Fort Worth Press*, researched the role of political pundits and wrote the following in the TPA's *Texas Press Messenger*:

> The press before and during the Texas Republic (1836–1845) was a free press in every sense of the word. Its editors were rugged personalities, with virile words on the tips of their pens. When they disagreed with a citizen or politician they went at once to the point to call him "a grump-headed footlick," a "dirty wretch" or a "premeditated malignant calumniator" and "foul-mouth liar"—even referring to highest government dignitaries as imbeciles and hog thieves.

While the message may have been softened in the last century, the spirit of the earlier pundits was evident in the humorous writings of the late Archer Fullingim, editor and publisher of the *Kountze County News*. Perhaps the most outspoken liberal journalist in Texas during the 1950s and '60s, Fullingim, or "The Printer," as he preferred to be called, enjoyed poking fun at the Establishment while getting across his political points.

Depending on one's own political convictions, Fullingim's popularity or notoriety began to spread across the state during those fierce Democratic primary battles that preceded Texas becoming a two-party state.

In a typical column that appeared in April 1962, Fullingim expressed his views on the gubernatorial race between John Connally and Don Yarborough with humor that resounded far beyond his beloved Hardin County:

(Connally's) eyes are those of a man who has handled millions of dollars for other people . . . For governor, I'll take the man who runs his campaign on the donation from the town dogcatcher . . . I'm proud that "Red" Williams, the dogcatcher, was Yarborough's first contributor here.

When his newspaper reached a circulation of 1,000 in 1954, Fullingim made it clear he was a small-time publisher and wanted to keep it that way.

The paid circulation of the *Kountze News* reached 1,000 last week for the first time . . . That's pretty good when you consider that the *News* had to give papers away the first six weeks of its life in September and October of 1950.

This printer figures that now just about everybody in the Kountze and Honey Island area is reading the paper. As soon as we get everybody in the Village Mills and Saratoga area taking the paper, we are not going to take anymore subscriptions . . . I'll be durned if I'm going to stand up there and feed that press for more than 3 hours at a time.

Today, Molly Ivins, the nationally syndicated political columnist for the *Fort Worth Star-Telegram* and perhaps the most widely read Texas journalist, continues the art of rolling politics and humor into the same ball of yarn. The former editor of the *Texas Observer* sees politics, particularly the Texas style, as "great entertainment" according to her profile on the *Star-Telegram*'s Web site. "(It is) better than the zoo, better than the circus, rougher than football, and even more aesthetically satisfying than baseball."

Ivins, who grew up in Houston, also has worked for the *New York Times*, *Houston Chronicle*, *Minneapolis Star-Tribune*, and the late *Dallas Times Herald*. She has been a Pulitzer Prize finalist numerous times and is the author of *Molly Ivins Can't Say That, Can She?* among other books. The answer is she can and does. In a column about the congressional redistricting fight in Texas in the summer and fall of 2003, Ivins wrote:

Charles Dickens' Mr. Bumble observed that the law is an ass, and he'd never even seen the . . . plan drawn by Texas Republicans. Sigh. I hate it when Tom DeLay and Karl Rove get away with a dirty deal like this. The University of Texas is now represented by Lamar Smith of San Antonio; I'm in a district that runs to the Mexican border; and two blocks north of me, they're in with Houston. Help.

While political humor in Texas newspapers has had a presence of more than a century and a half, levity in sports sections is relatively new, dating back to the 1950s when a young writer named Blackie Sherrod returned from World War II and joined the *Fort Worth Press*.

Sherrod flashed a style that soon would be copied, but never improved upon, by countless sportswriters throughout the nation. And from Doctor Sherrod's own laboratory deep in the bowels of the fun-loving *Press*, came the likes of Dan Jenkins, Bud Shrake, and Gary Cartwright. His influence also was obvious in Houston and San Antonio, where young writers like Mickey Herskowitz of the *Houston Post* (now a *Chronicle* columnist) and Dan Cook of the *Express-News* began to recognize the lighter side of sports. After Sherrod left the *Press* to join the *Dallas Times Herald* and then jumped to the *Dallas Morning News*, a young Skip Bayless followed in Sherrod's footsteps at the *Times Herald*. And today Fort Worth is not without an excellent press-box pundit, in the form of the *Star-Telegram*'s Randy Galloway.

Sherrod, who retired from the *News* in 2003, says his inspiration for making sports more entertaining came after joining the *Press* and soon discovering that as a sports editor and columnist he was facing two situations that would have to be addressed. One was competing against the *Star-Telegram*, with its larger staff, larger news hole, and solid readership hold on just about every acre west of Cowtown. The other was television.

Sherrod realized that television, though in its infancy, was going to have a major impact on the way people followed sports. He also deduced that most homes had only one television set and that the man of the house, in an era of undiluted chauvinism, would control what was on the screen. Largely it was sports.

Sherrod decided to introduce bright, attractive, and humorous writing into the sports department, hoping it would attract female readers who were the nightly hostages to television baseball, football, and wrestling.

"Walter Humphrey was editor of the *Press*, and he would let us get away with just about anything," Sherrod said.

Sherrod's idea was to cover sporting events and personalities in a wry way without forsaking any of the accuracy and drama involved in the action on the field.

Instead of writing that Arkansas coach Bowen Wyatt was upset over his team losing a close football game, Sherrod would write: "It was enough to make Wyatt Urp."

And when a Fort Worth Cats pitcher named Bob Austin pitched a no-hit game in the Texas League, Sherrod remained humorously skeptical. "If he is so good, why don't we name the state capital for him?" he wrote. Cartwright recalls the irreverence Sherrod championed. "Sportswriters everywhere else protected and created images false to the jocks we were writing about," he said. "Blackie taught us to tell it like it was. Yogi Berra wasn't this clever guy always ready with a quip, but a noncommunicative little fart whose funniest line was something like 'How the hell should I know?'"

In a 2003 *Texas Monthly* tribute to his mentor, Cartwright wrote that working for Sherrod was an exercise of wit and will.

The master hated idle hands and organized track meets in the sports departments of the old *Fort Worth Press* and later the *Dallas Times Herald*. We arm-wrestled, performed push-ups on the composing room floor, chin-ups in the men's room, and 50-yard dashes on the way to breakfast. Between editions we read aloud to each other—Runyon, Ring Lardner, Dorothy Parker, James Thurber, S. J. Perelman.

Blackie's distinctive brand of sarcasm and above-the-fray attitude molded us as young writers, made us appreciate that sports writing, done correctly, was broader than a playing field. Nothing was sacred; no one was spared. At a time when newspapers were reporting the scandalous affair of Ingrid Bergman and director Roberto Rossellini, Blackie saw it as a handy metaphor for a Texas League anomaly. He wrote: 'The Fort Worth Cats, like Miss Ingrid Bergman, play very well away from home.'

By his own tough, erudite, highly distinctive style he taught us to break the mold, to think out of the box, to take chances. News stories must transcend facts, stretching instead for style and analysis.

Because of the long-standing rivalry between Dallas and Fort Worth, it should come as no surprise that newspapers in the two cities tried for years to outdo each other in promoting "front page" columnists whose five- or six-day-a-week contributions contained heavy elements of humor. Two of these were Paul Crume of the *Dallas Morning News* and George Dolan of the *Fort Worth Star-Telegram*.

Crume joined the *News* in 1936, straight out of the University of Texas, and wrote his famous "Big D" column from 1952 until his death in 1975. According to a story written by Brian Anderson for the *News*'s DMN, the column was an experiment to see if Crume could bring a personal touch to the paper's front page.

Describing Crume's style in the same article, Ann Atterberry, who retired from the *News* in 1999 after thirty-six years as a writer and editor, said, "He was a wordsmith extraordinaire. His columns were folksy but also had a feel of sophistication."

Crume seemed to enjoy being the butt of his own jokes. Born in a log cabin and possessing a striking resemblance to Abraham Lincoln, Crume once wrote, "Despite this promising start, it is as near as I ever came to the presidency."

Mrs. Atterberry recalled to Anderson how Crume "would spend the day walking the hallways, pondering his chosen topics for hours before finally putting his creations to paper at the last possible moment. He paced a lot while he put his thoughts together. He did it (writing) more in his head than at his typewriter."

Although humor was his main game, Crume's 1967 column about the omnipresence of angels around us is his most famous piece of writing—so much so that the *News* reruns "To Touch an Angel" each year around Christmas. An excerpt:

> Any adult human being with half sense, and some with more, knows that there are angels. If he has ever spent any period in loneliness, when the senses are forced in upon themselves, he has felt the wind from their beating wings and been overwhelmed with the sudden realization of the endless and gigantic dark that exists outside the little candle flame of human knowledge.

In Fort Worth, Dolan was king for more than thirty years. Louie Hulme, who edited a collection of his friend's columns for a 1989 book titled *The Best and the Rest of George Dolan*, said Dolan "basically wrote about human nature in the Southwest."

"He picked out the funny side and the funny side tended to reveal all the other sides," Hulme wrote on the inside cover of the book.

Dolan's roaring laughter was his calling card. Also writing for the Dolan book, Blackie Sherrod said, "The man can curse louder and in the next breath, laugh longer than any Irisher in captivity." Jack Tinsley, the late *Star-Telegram* news executive, said that Dolan was a truly humorous man. "Dolan was always giggling, in his early days, even when he was taking obit information over the phone," Tinsley added.

Dolan also was one of several *Star-Telegram* writers—including Jerry Flemmons, Jim Trinkle, and Rich Richhart—who once created and promoted a fictional baseball team known as the Fort Worth Strangers. The gag lasted long enough for CBS to send in a television crew to cover the phenomenon, and it was reported to the nation by none other than Walter Cronkite.

Currently, the funny side of life as depicted in Texas newspapers could be described as "more hip" and "with it". An easily understood comparison would be between the writing of Ken Hoffman in the *Houston Chronicle* today and the work of Allison Sanders, the *Chronicle*'s "Motorman" columnist of the

1950s and '60s. Hoffman, as did Sanders, fundamentally relies on a short-take style, covering several topics in one day's column, but Hoffman's territory includes food, music, sports, or just about anything relating to pop culture.

But, who is to say that Sanders's writing did not reflect the culture of his era—a period when family values were held in higher esteem than they are today? His were the days of Ozzie and Harriet, a period when "Hey, Mabel, you gotta read this . . ." was a familiar living-room expression. Hoffman's audience wants to read more about Ozzy Osbourne, and "Yo!" is today's favorite attention-getting expression.

Hoffman believes his popularity has developed because he tries to go in many different directions in a given day. "My idea for a successful column is to have something there for everyone," he said.

He also writes a nationally syndicated fast-food column, "The Drive-Thru Gourmet," which is loaded down with as many laughs as calories, and he has served as a comedy writer for a number of radio stations across the nation.

His 1999 book is titled *Ken Hoffman: You Want Fries with That?* In his introduction he describes the "Hoffman style" of writing better than anyone else will ever be able to:

> I've always had fun with my newspaper column. It has allowed me to do things and go places and meet people I never dreamed of.
>
> I've whacked tennis balls with Bjorn Borg and John McEnroe and Chris Evert. I scored five points for the Washington Generals against the Harlem Globetrotters. I've shagged fly balls with my boyhood hero Willie Mays. I have been body-slammed by too many professional wrestlers to count.
>
> I've slept huddled under animal skins, in a teepee near the Arctic Circle, and counted stars in the Australian sky. I've traveled to the Orient to meet the greatest inventor of the twentieth century. No. Not some computer geek. The man who invented the Whoopee Cushion and the Dribble Glass.

That's Hoffman and some of the best humor around today. His compositions set you up, make you ponder, and then pow! The knockout punch!

But thinking it over . . . maybe that has been the aim of Texas newspaper humorists all along.

JACK LOFTIS, *the editor emeritus of the* Houston Chronicle, *began his newspaper career in 1955 as a sportswriter in his hometown of Hillsboro, Texas. He joined the* Chronicle *as a copy editor in 1965 and retired in 2002 as editor and associate publisher. Loftis and wife Beverly divide their time between homes in Houston and Lake Conroe.*

CHAPTER 12

The Impact of Technology on Texas Newspapers

WAYNE DANIELSON

Technology has affected Texas newspapers over the last century both by changing the way they gather, produce, and publish the news and by raising up a variety of new competitors eager to make money by distributing the news in new ways. Newspapers have moved from telegraph to telephone, from hot type to cold type, and from traditional to computerized production methods. They have made these changes at the same time that they were adjusting to the advent of motion pictures, radio, television, and, in recent years, the mysterious and vaguely threatening Internet.

STABLE TIMES

Although a great deal of change has occurred in newspaper publishing in the twentieth century, most of that change seems to have happened in the last half of the century. In journalism schools during the 1950s, for example, it was commonly observed that printers from the previous century could have gone right to work in most newspaper composing rooms. They would have felt right at home.

Change had taken place, of course, but not all that much. The Linotype, the ahead-of-its-times publishing miracle of the late nineteenth century, was still there, clicking and clacking away, only a little bit faster than it had been years before. You ran it now with perforated tape that had been pioneered during the 1940s by the *Abilene Reporter-News* and neighboring newspapers.

Presses were much the same as they had been, only faster. The huge impact of cold type and offset printing still lay in the future for many newspapers.

Reporters and editors relied on mechanical typewriters whose keyboards and "touch" would have been familiar to journalists of fifty years earlier;

electric typewriters were considered expensive and perhaps a little fragile for newspaper work.

Newspapers ran on paper and ink and lead, and stories passed from hand to hand from reporter to copy desk, to composition, to page makeup, to printing, and, eventually, to circulation.

In the business offices, clerks and managers worked with ledgers and papers, typewriters and filing cabinets, with a few mechanical or electric adding machines thrown in to help balance the accounts. With a few quick lessons on a few new devices, Dickens's Ebenezer Scrooge would have felt right at home in those offices.

Computers had been invented, but were seldom to be found as yet on the news side of most newspapers, and electronic networks connecting the various divisions of the newspaper had yet to be invented.

Publishers, although they didn't oppose technological change, did insist that any proposed change contribute substantially to the efficient and profitable operation of the enterprise. Unless a clear case could be made for a new technology, it was unlikely to be adopted.

"Should we bother to go online?" a Texas publisher once called to ask me one day in the late 1990s. "Is the online newspaper going to amount to anything?"

"I don't know," I replied. "I'm not sure how it much income it will generate. But it has possibilities. Why don't you start in a small way? You'll be ahead of your competitors if anything important happens."

That's what he and many other Texas publishers did. When they could, they made experimental investments in online technologies. They put their foot in the door and waited to see what would happen. If results proved to be promising, as they often did, publishers made larger investments, and change ensued. If results were questionable, not much harm had been done. Pioneers had to pay large prices for new technology, whereas those who waited often benefited from rapidly declining costs.

COMPETING MEDIA

Printing with movable type is considered by some historians to be the ancestor of all mass production. Most newspaper publishers certainly would have agreed with that generous interpretation of the importance of their contribution to society. And in truth, getting out a finished printed product every day or every week was an impressive accomplishment. Efficient, tightly organized, and well-managed newspapers in full production were modern miracles, something to behold.

More than a little satisfaction existed in an industry that had changed the way the nation's workers worked, and publishers were understandably resistant to the rise of upstart competitors. In their time, the new media of radio, facsimile (now called fax machines), television, computers, and the Internet faced opposition from newspapers, but managed to endure and prosper without hurting the papers in the process. Indeed, many publishers decided early on that their policy would be "If you can't beat 'em, buy 'em!" And to the extent permitted by the law, that is exactly what they did. And that is why the initials of many radio and television stations contain references to their origins in print journalism. WGN in Chicago stands no doubt for "World's Greatest Newspaper," the slogan of the *Chicago Tribune*.

In July 1933, a writer in the *Texas Press Messenger* expressed doubt that "radio homes" had really reached 16,809,562, as reported by the Columbia Broadcasting Company. The writer gloomily observed that radios wear out and cease to work, and "many are being set out by the curb and thrown away, never to be replaced!" Take that, Columbia Broadcasting Company!

Paul J. Thompson, then head of journalism at the University of Texas, wondered in the March 1933 *Messenger* whether a "radio typewriter" or facsimile machine would become commonplace in American homes. That did happen, eventually, with copiers and computer printers, but not for many years. Of television, which much more quickly became a much bigger competitor for advertising dollars, he said almost as an aside, "Television is being talked about here."

Publishers also worried about the impact of new technology on the quality of newspapers. Some thought that faster or easier did not necessarily mean better. Kenneth Byerly, a weekly newspaper publisher in Montana and author of *Community Journalism*, doubted that computers would have a positive impact. While we were both serving on the faculty of the University of North Carolina School of Journalism, he challenged me to a journalistic shootout in a small town of my choosing.

"You take your computer, and I'll take a drunken printer and a flatbed press," He said. "And I'll have you out of business in six months."

He was undoubtedly right at the time, and I wisely declined the challenge. But later his opinion changed, as did the opinions of many publishers as well, as they observed the savings in labor that computerized typesetting promised. In the continuing battle between man and machine, John Henry had clearly lost again.

Although it dutifully noted the conflicts swirling about technological change, the *Texas Press Messenger*, throughout the century, seemed to take a forward-looking stance on the contributions technology was making and would make to newspaper publishing. It was always careful, however, to investigate and report on the costs of the equipment when it could.

The new machines might be amazing, but were they practical? The *Texas Press Messenger* in May 1943 called on publishers to "Send in your ideas that have been *proven by actual use*" (emphasis added).

It seems odd today, but it was not unusual in the early part of the twentieth century for newspapers to operate without telephones in the newsroom, or at least with very few.

As late as 1932, Southwestern Bell took out an advertisement in the May issue of the *Messenger* to tout the value of telephones for reporters. The advertisement recounted in detail the role the telephone had played in helping reporters communicate the story of Gerald Collins, a three-year-old who had fallen into a drill hole.

In the midst of the Great Depression, TPA President R. L. Scott of DeLeon advised his fellow publishers in the January 1932 edition of the *Messenger*: "There's still money to be made in the printing game. We must face the future with new plans and practice thrift and economy in a more intense fashion."

Publishers worried about the cost of new technology. Where would they get the money for such expensive machines? Would they get a worthwhile return on their investment?

During World War II, thrifty Texas publishers narrowed column widths and page sizes and kept old equipment in service as a contribution to the war effort. The April 1944 edition of the *Messenger* reported that a 106-year-old handpress was finally being retired at the *Palo Pinto County Star* where it had been in service for sixty-eight years. Actually, the story said, the old press would not go to the junk heap. It would continue to be used as a proof press!

Publishers worried about finding or training employees who knew how to use the new technologies, and they looked back in envy at the days when perfectly competent printers would just appear at the door, eager to go to work. They often found it, even though the *Messenger* wrote that one of them confessed to his prospective employer, "I'm just a durned drunk." In the February 1952 *Messenger*, Will C. Grant, director of the Southwest School of Printing in Dallas, recommended that publishers send at least one boy through printing school.

"Records show," he said, "that 1,500 printers are dying every year" and "only 1,000 of these printers are being replaced."

"The implication is obvious," he said.

At the same time that publishers were worrying about the high cost of technological change, they were taking pride in the new machines they had acquired. They invited fellow publishers to come and take a look at what they had installed.

The January 1952 *Messenger* covered an open house held by the *San Angelo Times* to celebrate its new $220,000 plant.

The paper reported that its new, sixty-four-page Universal Goss Press had its own foundation featuring precompressed cork pads.

"It is possible to stand three feet from the press foundation without feeling vibration," the *Messenger* said.

The story also reported that reporters and editors at the *Times* could exchange messages via pneumatic tubes with the composing room.

In March 1952 the *Messenger* reported that "ready print" inside pages for newspapers were being discontinued as of March 29. The money-saving commodity went back to Civil War days.

In the same issue, the *Waco News-Tribune* announced the installation of a Fairchild Scanagraver and a Teletypesetter, and the *Corpus Christi Caller-Times* reported that it had installed a Blue Streak Comet Linotype.

In the April 22, 1952, *Messenger*, Basson Nelson published a list of all the machinery needed to publish a newspaper. Surprisingly, it didn't take up much space.

Publishers were always aware of the financial advantages of having the technology in their own shops. They kept up with what was available by attending the A&M–TPA Mechanical and Photography Conference at College Station. For example, the March 1962 meeting emphasized the most recent developments in color printing.

Graphic Electronics demonstrated the Photo Lathe, a machine that produced half tones, line engravings, and reverse plates on plastic, magnesium, and zinc. The company reported that Klischograph Southwest at Hamilton, Texas, now made engravings in its home plant.

MORE RAPID CHANGE

The last half of the century was dominated by rapid technological changes in typesetting devices, printing plates, and presses as well as the widespread use of computers in all aspects of newspaper publishing.

The 1970s probably saw the most rapid change. At the beginning of the decade, a small percentage of Texas newspapers used photo-offset production, so-called cold type. By the end of the decade, a large majority had switched to the new printing method. Most newspaper change happens by evolution, not revolution. But by any fair measure the 1970s changes *were* revolutionary.

The adoption of computers in the 1980s and 1990s, though certainly as sweeping in its impact on Texas papers as the changes of the 1970s, seemed nevertheless to be more gradual. All of society was participating in these changes—not just the publishing industry—and perhaps the universality of the change mitigated the perception of rapid change in the industry.

Computers are generalized machines that work optimally with redundancy, and publishing newspapers is a highly redundant business. You can't make a new paper "from scratch" every time you publish. Familiar, predictable formats or patterns guide the process. Newspapers use the same machines over and over again. They use the same typefaces. They produce the same familiar sections and pages. They use "standing heads" to call attention to familiar columns. Readers turn to their papers expecting to find the same general kinds of news in the same place in the paper day after day. They learn the names and habits of individual writers and editors. The last thing a mother wants, for example, is for her daughter's wedding story to be "different." She wants it to be like all the other wedding stories—just bigger, and printed at the top of the page.

Although computers have seldom been used to write the more redundant stories–although they could probably do this—they have been widely used to search for other redundancies in newspaper operations and reduce them. As a result of increased computer use, papers are neater and more uniform in appearance and more economical to produce. Another result has been the gradual increase in online newspapers—papers constantly updated on the Internet as new stories come in. Ready or not, newspapers have found themselves back in the "speed game" again, with the possibility arising of competing head-to-head with radio and TV in the timeliness of their offerings.

Most Texas newspapers originally hoped to fill their "electronic columns" cheaply with stories produced as part of normal operating procedures, but new media tend to require new methods, and greater differences in the online products are now apparent. New and imaginative ways of presenting the news on smaller and more color-filled pages seem to be resulting in products that look less and less like traditional papers. The new papers are livelier and scrappier. Rapid feedback from readers seems to facilitate more rapid formation of public opinion, possibly increasing the power of the press. *Will* the paperless papers have more weight and influence than their predecessors? No one knows for sure now. But they may do very well in the long run with the new generation of keyboard- and computer-oriented young people now coming into positions of power and leadership.

WAYNE DANIELSON, *emeritus professor of journalism and computer science at the University of Texas at Austin, began his professional career in 1953 as a reporter at the* San Jose Mercury-News, *where he later served as research manager. He earned a PhD in mass communication research at Stanford University in 1957.*

He has served as dean of the School of Journalism at the University of North Carolina at Chapel Hill and as dean of the College of Communication at UT Austin. His teaching interests include news writing, editing, and computer applications in journalism.

The Press

NELLIE PAGET

Dedicated to the Texas Press Association. Read at the El Paso meeting, 1889.

When historians of the future write the story of today,
And inscribe in "shining record," the parts which heroes play,
The sword will not be glorified, nor be debased the pen—
And the men who lead the vanguard will receive their guerdon then.

The reign of force is over—'tis forever left behind;
The battles of the present are but conflicts of the mind,
And the mightiest of warrior hosts that for the battle dress,
Are as pigmies to the men who hold the "thunders of the Press."

This Herculean civilizer knows no repulse nor fear;
It does its work, it speaks its will, and all the earth must hear,
And the editor, so late despised—the butt of many a jest—
Now finds a way where monarchs fail to do the Right's behest.

From pole to pole, from sea to sea, unmoved by fire or flood,
Undaunted, brave, persistent, free alike with wealth of blood,
The Agents of the Press are found, where noble work's to do—
And the world ne'er knows the hardships of these men to duty true.

In the burning sands of Africa a Livingston is lost,
Midst the arctic's dreadful snowdrifts a Greeley, too, is tossed;
There is grief in all the nations for those brave men unmourned as dead,
But the Press sends out its searchers and the rest you all have read.

In every field of Action, and in every line of thought,
The Press is Avant Courrieur and with mighty prowess fraught;
'Tis the poor man's "court of last resort" and lends a willing ear
To all appeals the people make, unswayed by greed or fear.

The power is felt and recognized, "in court, and camp, and hall,"
Soldier, statesman, commoner, king, the Press does lead them all;
Actor, preacher, politician, and the "merchant prince," no less,
Owe their fame and many "shekels" to the "minions of the Press."

It can build a town or make a man, or unmake both at will—
Its Merlin-wand, the pencil, hath the power to save or kill;
It can help the struggling forward, it can check oppression's sway,
And the tyrant's will is thwarted when the Press doth bar the way.

Then be true each valiant brother to each purpose great and good—
Unite your wondrous forces for Universal Brotherhood—
Till rejuvenated earth shall rise and life its voice and bless
The bulwark of our freedom—a free, untrammeled Press.

NELLIE PAGET *was the wife of O. Paget of the* Corsicana Courier. *Printed proceedings from early TPA conventions reveal that it was customary for one of the ladies present to read or recite a poem.*

Fast Facts

* O. B. Colquitt, elected governor of Texas in 1911, was the founder of the *Pittsburgh Gazette*.

* Will H. Mayes, publisher of the *Brownwood Bulletin*, was president of the Texas Press Association in 1899. He was the first newspaperman to also serve as Texas lieutenant governor, elected in 1912. He served one term, and then served as dean of the department of journalism at the University of Texas until 1925.

* Allen Shivers, Texas governor from 1950 to 1957, was a co-owner of the *Mission Times*.

* Price Daniel, U.S. senator from 1953 to 1957 and Texas governor from 1957 to 1963, owned the *Liberty Vindicator*. His son, Price Daniel Jr., was speaker of the Texas House in 1973.

* Bill Hobby, executive editor and president of his family's newspaper, the *Houston Post*, was Texas lieutenant governor from 1973 to 1991.

* State senator Chet Brooks was a *Houston Post* reporter and worked for TPA before serving thirty years in the Texas Legislature as a state representative and state senator.

* In 1969, three newsmen served in the Texas House of Representatives: George Baker, publisher of the *Fort Stockton Pioneer*; Jack Hawkins, publisher of the *Groesbeck Journal*; and Dave Allred, a reporter for the *Wichita Falls Times*.

* Prior to 1836 there were only ten newspapers in Texas. General James Long made the first attempt at publishing with the *Texas Republican*, printed in Nacogdoches in 1819. In 1880, the year the Texas Press Association was organized, there were 264 newspapers in Texas: 30 dailies, 1 triweekly, 2 semiweeklies, and 231 weeklies.

* In 1865, only eight daily newspapers were published in Texas; four of them were in Galveston. At various times between 1876 and 1890, twenty-three newspapers were published in Galveston. When the *Galveston News* was established in 1842, it was the twenty-seventh newspaper to appear in Texas. In 1968, the *Galveston News* installed new presses and became the state's largest offset newspaper. Today, it is the oldest, continually published newspaper in the state.

* During the Civil War, newspapers were printed on rice paper, straw paper, wrapping paper, and wallpaper.

* Ellis and Montague counties had press associations of their own in 1893. Each had several newspapers.

* At its 1891 convention in Corsicana, the Texas Press Association kicked off a project that ultimately brought about the state's purchase of the San Jacinto battleground, site of the pivotal battle in Texas's war for independence. Judge A. B. Norton led TPA members in the effort that inspired the Legislature to buy the land and create the state park.

* In 1899, another TPA project resulted in the founding of the College of Industrial Arts in Denton. Today, that college is Texas Woman's University.

* The Texas Legislature passed the state's first civil libel law in 1901, working with TPA members who said the final draft was "not perfect, but a step in the right direction."

* Humble Oil founder and one-time newspaperman Ross S. Sterling was the first candidate to use the Texas Press Association to place ads in selected newspapers during his campaign for governor in 1930. Twenty years later, the TPA placed $77,000 in political advertising. Today, the TPA places upwards of $500,000 in candidate advertising in member newspapers. Ads for constitutional amendments can account for as much as $900,000 in legislative years.

Ross Sterling delivers his inaugural speech as Governor of Texas, 1931. *Courtesy William P. Hobby Sr. Family Papers, Center for American History, The University of Texas at Austin.*

★ Oveta Culp Hobby of the *Houston Post* publishing family was the first director of the Women's Army Corps. In 1945, she received the Distinguished Service Medal.

★ The federal minimum wage increased from 75 cents to $1 an hour in 1956. Newspapers with circulation below 4,000 were exempt from the federal law.

★ Joe Galloway of the United Press International was the first reporter from Texas assigned to cover the Vietnam War. Galloway got his start at the *Refugio County Press*, where he worked for C. M. "Cap" Henkel.

★ Governor John Connally signed the Texas Open Meetings Law into effect on May 23, 1967, more than twenty years after the TPA began lobbying for the legislation. In 1973, Governor Dolph Briscoe signed the Open Records Act, which is now known as the Texas Public Information Act.

Governor Dolph Briscoe Jr. and his wife Janey in his office in Uvalde, Texas. *From the Prints and Photographs Collection, Center for American History, The University of Texas at Austin. CN Number 00827 a, b.*

* Speakers at the 1974 TPA Mid-Winter convention included top-ranking state officials, including Governor Dolph Briscoe, Lieutenant Governor Bill Hobby, Attorney General John Hill, House Speaker Price Daniel Jr., and Secretary of State Mark White. U.S. Senator John Tower was also on the agenda.

* In 1978, state comptroller Bob Bullock told the TPA convention attendees that property taxes averaged $213 a person, warning that "the time is ripe for tax relief, tax reforms and to consider tax limitations."

TPA Executive Directors

ED STERLING

After World War II, Texas Press Association members realized that the association could not exist as a volunteer, do-it-when-you-have-time organization. Groundwork was finally laid for establishing a full-time business office and employing an experienced, highly qualified general manager.

In its long history, TPA has had only four managers:

Vernon T. (Vern) Sanford, 1947–1971
W. G. (Bill) Boykin, 1971–1974
Lyndell Williams, 1974–1998
Micheal Hodges, 1998–present

On November 30, 1947, Vern Sanford became the first, full-time general manager of TPA. Sanford previously had spent thirteen years as head of the Oklahoma Press Association.

Sanford ran the TPA out of a hotel room at the Baker Hotel in Dallas until September 1948, when the association headquarters moved to Austin, first to the Driskill Hotel, then to a suite of offices at the International Life Insurance Building, and then to a small, frame house at 18th and San Antonio near the University of Texas campus.

He managed TPA for twenty-four years until his retirement in 1971.

Bill Boykin succeeded Sanford at TPA, after a newspaper career in Oklahoma and serving as executive director of the Florida Press Association. He arrived at TPA in September 1970 as Sanford's understudy, and was named TPA general manager nine months later.

Boykin oversaw TPA's move into its current headquarters at 718 West Fifth Street in Austin, the former home of a soft-drink bottling plant.

Just three years later, when Boykin left Texas to become executive director of the Inland Press Association, TPA again looked to Oklahoma for leadership talent. Hiring the Oklahoma Press Association assistant manager, Lyndell Williams, as the third TPA general manager was heralded as "one of the most significant events in the history of the Texas Press Association."

Williams began his twenty-four-year tenure by working closely with the membership to retire a $35,000 debt. After stabilizing the association's finances, he continued to manage conservatively, with an emphasis on building cash reserves. By the time he retired in June 1998, he had cut waste and managed the association's investments into a portfolio worth more than $2 million.

While brightening the association's financial picture, Williams introduced regularly scheduled activities for the sole benefit of members, including an annual trade show, advertising short courses, and newswriting clinics. He ushered in the computer era at the central office in Austin by outfitting the building with networked workstations and by overseeing the conversion of an upstairs boardroom into a computer-equipped classroom for the training of members in the use of software such as Adobe Photoshop and QuarkXpress.

Also of note was Williams's relationship with the late Bob Bullock, then Texas comptroller of public accounts. Williams quietly earned Bullock's confidence through meetings and telephone calls, eventually convincing the statesman of the legislature's error in passing a tax on newspaper circulation in 1983. Bullock's influence played a big part in the repeal of the tax in 1987, and he became widely regarded as a "friend of the press" while serving as lieutenant governor from 1991 through 1998.

Micheal R. Hodges, a native of Crosbyton, succeeded Williams in 1998. Hodges, who had served as TPA's director of advertising since 1991, was the first native Texan to fill the role of full-time manager of the association.

Hodges developed a strong work ethic while growing up on his family's cotton farm and continuing in that line of work into early adulthood. He earned a bachelor's degree in business from West Texas State University in 1977 and then found work selling advertising for a radio station in Borger. This position soon led Hodges to the *Canyon News*. Publisher Brad Tooley saw potential and hired Hodges as advertising manager. After two years of seasoning in that competitive market, Hodges was hired as a group advertising manager by DFW Suburban Newspapers in the Dallas–Fort Worth Metroplex. Hodges secured employment as a group manager for a newspaper chain in suburban St. Louis.

In 1991, the position of director of advertising opened at TPA. Williams called Hodges and invited him to apply. Hodges, excited at the opportunity to return to Texas, interviewed, received an offer, and accepted it. While serving as advertising director, Hodges converted the Texas Newspaper Advertising Bureau into a more efficient and effective vehicle for advertising. He personally solicited major retail accounts while building the Texas Statewide Classified Advertising Network and the Campaign Advertising Program from the ground up.

Hodges launched an aggressive program of updates and upgrades to the central office, including a major reconfiguration of the floor space and the display of artifacts and historical photographs. He also engineered the sale of the Texas Press Clipping Service, a long-term adjunct operation of the association, to Geotel Corporation of Missouri.

Among many accomplishments in Hodges's plan to improve member services were the equipping of a mobile classroom deployed regularly to sites across Texas, on the request of dues-paying members, and the offering of on-demand workshops in a wide range of topics to meet the specific needs of members.

Hodges also worked with the College of Communication at Texas Christian University to develop the Community Journalism Project, a training forum for midcareer journalists underwritten by the Texas Newspaper Foundation. Likewise, Hodges was instrumental in developing joint online journalism training programs with the School of Journalism at the University of Texas at Austin.

TPA Presidents

TERM	PRESIDENT
1880–1881	J. W. Fishburn *Mexia Ledger*
1881–1882	H. L. Gosling *Castroville Quill*
1882–1883	H. L. Gosling *Castroville Quill*
1883–1884	W. M. Yandell *Seguin Times*
1884–1885	W. L. Hall *Dallas Herald*
1885–1886	T. J. Girardeau* *Houston Journal*
1886	J. H. Davis *Mount Vernon Herald*
1886–1887	L. L. Foster *Limestone New Era*
1887–1888	William Ferguson *San Antonio Times*

did not complete term of office

1888–   J. P. Bridges
1889   *Luling Signal*

1889–   R. M. Johnston
1890   *Houston Post*

1890–   Juan S. Hart
1891   *El Paso Times*

1891–   J. F. Mitchell
1892   *Greenville Banner*

1892–   John H. Copeland
1893   *San Antonio News*

1893–   A. C. Scurlock
1894   *Cleburne Chronicle*

1894–   Frank P. Holland
1895   *Texas Farm & Ranch* (Austin)

1895–   W. W. Adair
1896   *Marshall Messenger*

1896   John H. Cullom
         Garland News

1896–   F. B. Baillio
1897   *Cleburne Review*

1897–   S. M. Vernon
1898   *Comanche Chief*

1898–   John G. Rankin
1899   *Brenham Banner*

1899–   William H. Mayes
1900   *Brownwood Bulletin*

1900–   E. W. Harris
1901   *Greenville Herald*

1901–   F. B. Robinson
1902   *Huntsville Item*

1902–   C. N. Ousley
1903   *Houston Post*

1903–   R. E. Yantis
1904   *Athens Review*

1904–   Sidney J. Thomas
1905   *Comanche Chief*

1905–   J. H. Lowry
1906   *Honey Grove Signal*

1906–   Thomas W. Perkins
1907   *McKinney Courier-Gazette*

1907–   W. J. Buie
1908   *Waxahachie Enterprise*

1908–   C. E. Gilmore
1909   *Wills Point Chronicle*

1909–   W. A. Johnson
1910   *Memphis Herald*

1910–   J. R. Ransone Jr.
1911   *Cleburne Enterprise*

1911–   J. A. Thomas
1912   *Mineola Monitor*

1912–   W. C. Edwards
1913   *Denton Record-Chronicle*

1913– Joe J. Taylor
1914   *Dallas Morning News*

1914– D. R. Harris
1915   *Rusk County News*

1915– Walter B. Whitman
1916   *Holland's Magazine* (Dallas)

1916– Henry P. Edwards
1917   *Troup Banner*

1917– Sherwood Spotts
1918   *Bonham Favorite*

1918– Harry Koch
1919   *Quanah Tribune-Chief*

1919– Sam Fore Jr.
1920   *Floresville Chronicle-Journal*

1920– John Esten Cooke
1921   *Rockdale Reporter*

1921– Judd Mortimer Lewis
1922   *Houston Chronicle*

1922– Denver Chesnutt
1923   *Kenedy Advance*

1923– Sam M. Braswell
1924   *Clarendon News*

1924– A. H. Luker
1925   *Grapeland Messenger*

1925– W. A. Smith
1926   *San Saba News*

| 1926– | R. L. Baldridge |
| 1927 | *Clifton Record* |

| 1927– | George A. T. Neu* |
| 1928 | *Brenham Banner* |

| 1928– | E. A. Carlock |
| 1928 | *Paducah Post* |

| 1928– | Sam E. Miller |
| 1929 | *Mineral Wells Index* |

| 1929– | Harry F. Schwenker |
| 1930 | *Brady Standard* |

| 1930– | R. H. Nichols |
| 1931 | *Vernon Record* |

| 1931– | R. L. Scott |
| 1932 | *DeLeon Free Press* |

| 1932– | Lowry Martin |
| 1933 | *Corsicana Sun* |

| 1933– | R. F. Higgs |
| 1934 | *Stephenville Empire-Tribune* |

| 1934– | Sam C. Holloway |
| 1935 | *Deport Times* |

| 1935– | Louis C. Elbert |
| 1936 | *Deport Times* |

| 1936– | H. H. Jackson |
| 1937 | *Coleman Democrat-Voice* |

| 1937– | R. J. Edwards |
| 1938 | *Denton Record-Chronicle* |

Texas Press Association past presidents; photo circa 1951. Front row (seated) from left: Sam Braswell, *Clarendon News*, 1923–24; L. M. Watson, *Sweetwater News*, 1943–44; Sam C. Holloway, *Deport Times*, 1934–35; R. H. Nichols, *Vernon Record*, 1930–31; Rufus Higgs, *Stephenville Empire-Tribune*, 1933–34; A. H. Luker, *Grapeland Messenger*, 1924–25. Backrow, from left: Van Stewart, *Ochiltree County Herald*, 1949–50; Fred Massengill Jr., *Terrell Tribune*, 1950–51; Dave M. Warren, *Panhandle Herald*, 1941–42; Walter Humphrey, *Fort Worth Press*, 1946–47; Charles K. Devall, *Kilgore News Herald*, 1940–41; Robert Matherne, *Baytown Sun*, 1948–49; Walter Buckner, *San Marcos Record*, 1939–40; Paul M. Fulks, *Wolfe City Sun*, 1947–48; Deskins Wells, *Wellington Leader*, 1938–39.

1938–1939	Deskins Wells *Wellington Leader*
1939–1940	Walter Buckner *San Marcos Record*
1940–1941	Charles K. Devall *Kilgore News Herald*
1941–1942	David M. Warren *Panhandle Herald*

1942– James F. Donahue
1943   *Freeport Facts-Review*

1943– Luther M. Watson
1944   *Sweetwater News*

1944– George B. Peeler
1945   *Taylor Daily Press*

1945– Joe T. Cook
1946   *Mission Times*

1946– Walter R. Humphrey
1947   *Fort Worth Press*

1947– Paul M. Fulks
1948   *Wolfe City Sun*

1948– Robert Matherne
1949   *Baytown Sun*

1949– Van W. Stewart
1950   *Ochiltree County Herald*

1950– Frederick I. Massengill Jr.
1951   *Terrell Tribune*

1951– Brad H. Smith
1952   *Weslaco News*

1952– William Rawland
1953   *Cleburne Times-Review*

1953– Arthur H. Kowert
1954   *Fredericksburg Standard*

1954– W. R. Beaumier
1955   *Lufkin Daily News*

1955–
1956
    Russell W. Bryant
    Italy News-Herald

1956–
1957
    David C. Leavell
    Galveston News-Tribune

1957–
1958
    Jimmie Gillentine
    Hereford Brand

1958–
1959
    J. C. Smyth
    Liberty Vindicator

1959–
1960
    Tom Whitehead Sr.
    Brenham Banner-Press

1960–
1961
    L. B. Smith
    Brady Standard-Herald

1961–
1962
    Victor B. Fain
    Nacogdoches Daily Sentinel

1962–
1963
    George Baker
    Fort Stockton Pioneer

1963–
1964
    William E. "Bill" Berger
    Hondo Anvil Herald

1964–
1965
    Aubrey McAllister
    Bonham Daily Favorite

1965–
1966
    Winn B. Crossley
    Madisonville Meteor

1966–
1967
    Jim Barnhill
    Hillsboro Daily Mirror

1967–
1968
    Harold Hudson
    Perryton Herald

1968– 1969	W. Glynn Morris *Borger News-Herald*
1969– 1970	George Hawkes *Arlington Citizen-Journal*
1970– 1971	Ellie Hopkins *Longview News and Journal*
1971– 1972	Rigby Owen Sr. *Conroe Courier*
1972– 1973	Don Coppedge *Waxahachie Daily Light*
1973– 1974	Tom Steely *Lamar County Echo*
1974– 1975	Glenn Sedam *Bay City Tribune*
1975– 1976	John Taylor *Seguin Gazette*
1976– 1977	J. C. Chatmas *Marlin Daily Democrat*
1977– 1978	Bob Hamilton *Iowa Park Leader*
1978– 1979	Fred V. Barbee Jr. *El Campo Leader-News*
1979– 1980	Bill Dozier *Kerrville Daily Times*
1980– 1981	James Roberts *Andrews County News*

1981– 1982	O. G. "Speedy" Nieman *Hereford Brand*
1982– 1983	T. H. "Hal" Cunningham *Llano News*
1983– 1984	John Crawford *Wood County Democrat*
1984– 1985	Frank Baker *Fort Stockton Pioneer*
1985– 1986	Walter Buckel *Lamesa Press Reporter*
1986– 1987	Charles Schulz *Taylor Daily Press*
1987– 1988	Roy Eaton *Wise County Messenger*
1988– 1989	Fred E. Lowe *Lampasas Dispatch Record*
1989– 1990	Roy McQueen *Snyder Daily News*
1990– 1991	Mary Henkel Judson *Port Aransas South Jetty*
1991– 1992	Christopher F. Barbee *El Campo Leader-News*
1992– 1993	Larry L. Crabtree *Vernon Daily Record*
1993– 1994	Jim Hudson *Perryton Herald*

1994–
1995
Dick Richards
Aransas Pass Progress

1995–
1996
Sarah L. Greene
Gilmer Mirror

1996–
1997
Jerry Tidwell
Hood County News

1997–
1998
Rollie Hyde
Plainview Daily Herald

1998–
1999
Larry Jackson
Wharton Journal-Spectator

1999–
2000
Lynn Brisendine
Brownfield News

2000–
2001
Alvin Holley
Polk County Publishing

2001–
2002
Larry Reynolds
Amarillo Globe-News

2002–
2003
Bob Buckel
Azle News

2003–
2004
Willis Webb
Jasper Newsboy

2004–
2005
Wanda Garner Cash
Baytown Sun

Featured Speakers at Texas Press Association Conventions

YEAR	SPEAKER
1948	Gavin Astor, assistant publisher, *Times* (London)
1949	Bishop Clinton S. Quin, Episcopal Diocese of Texas
1950	Governor Allan Shivers Charles H. Wiseman, Publisher's Idea Exchange (Des Moines, Iowa)
1951	Felix McKnight, *Dallas Morning News* Governor Allan Shivers Martin Dies, former U.S. congressman
1952	Governor Allan Shivers excursion to San Jacinto Battleground and Monument; *USS Texas*
1953	Senator James E. Taylor, former publisher, *Kerens Tribune*
1954	John Ben Shepperd, Texas Attorney General Oveta Culp Hobby, Secretary of Health, Education and Welfare Governor Allan Shivers
1955	Faye Lody, Dallas Bureau of UPI Ken Towery and Caro Brown, Pulitzer Prize winners Jim Lindsey, Speaker of the Texas House Vice President Richard M. Nixon

1956   Arthur H. "Red" Motley, publisher, *Parade Magazine*
       John Ben Shepperd, Texas Attorney General
       U.S. Senator Price Daniel
       Cal Farley, president, Cal Farley's Boys Ranch
       O. B. Ellis, general manager, Texas Prison System

1957   Will Wilson, Texas Attorney General
       William T. Rafael, Crusade for Freedom, New York
       Governor Price Daniel
       Waggoner Carr, Speaker of the Texas House

1958   Zollie Steakley, Texas Secretary of State
       Leo Aikman, *Atlanta Journal-Constitution*
       Tom Reavley, former Texas Secretary of State
       Governor Price Daniel
       Rear Admiral Charles Kirkpatrick, U.S. Navy

1959   Senator Hubert R. Hudson, Brownsville

1960   Virgil Hill, *Phoenix Gazette*
       John Henry Faulk
       Oveta Culp Hobby, *Houston Post*
       Vice President Richard M. Nixon

1961   Paul Richards, manager, Baltimore Orioles, winner of the first
          Texan of the Year Award
       Charles Corddry, editor, *Rockets and Missiles*

1962   Senator Culp Kreuger, *El Campo Leader-News*
       Van Cliburn, pianist, Texan of the Year Award
       Colonel Paul A. Campbell, Brooks Air Force Base, "Man in Space"

1963   Dan Blocker, actor, Texan of the Year Award
       John J. Peterson, NASA, "Manned Space Flight"

1964   Price Daniel, former governor, "The Press and the Law"
       DeWitt Reddick, Journalism Department, University of Texas
       Charles B. "Tex" Thornton, Texan of the Year Award
       U.S. Senator Ralph Yarborough
       George H. W. Bush, Republican candidate for U.S. Senate

1965   Eugene Cernan, U.S. astronaut, "America's Space Program"
Dr. Harry H. Ransom, chancellor, University of Texas system
Frederick C. Belen, Postmaster General

1966   Dale Evans, actress, Texan of the Year Award
Mac Sebree, UPI

1967   Allen Ludden, television personality, Texan of the Year Award
Leon Hale, *Houston Post*

1968   Raymond Berry, football star, Texan of the Year Award
W. Marvin Watson, Postmaster General

1969   Governor Preston Smith
Wick Fowler, U.S. ambassador to Vietnam

1970   Ken Towery, U.S. Information Agency, Washington, D.C.
Virginia Payette, United Features Syndicate, New York

1971   LBJ Ranch and home tour
Governor Preston Smith
Darwin Sharp, U.S. Postal Service, Washington, D.C.
Phyllis George, Miss America, Texan of the Year Award

1972   U.S. District Judge Sarah T. Hughes, Dallas
Chuck Bennett, Audit Bureau of Circulations, Chicago
U.S. Representative Jim Wright, Fort Worth
U.S. Representative Bob Casey, Houston
U.S. Representative Jim Collins, Dallas
U.S. Representative Graham Purcell, Wichita Falls
George Bush, U.S. Representative to the United Nations
U.S. Senator John Tower

1973   Governor Dolph Briscoe
Lieutenant Governor William Hobby Jr.
Price Daniel Jr., Speaker of the Texas House
U.S. Senator Lloyd Bentsen and congressional delegation
Robert Calvert, former Texas Chief Justice
Al Neuharth, president, Gannett Company Inc.

1974   U.S. Senator John Tower
        Governor Dolph Briscoe
        John Hill, Texas Attorney General
        Price Daniel, Speaker of the Texas House
        Mark White, Texas Secretary of State
        General Albert P. Clark, U.S. Air Force
        U.S. Senator Lloyd Bentsen

1975   Shirley Cothran, Miss America, Texan of the Year
        Bob Bullock, Texas Comptroller of Public Accounts
        Abe Lemons, basketball coach, University of Texas
        Helen Thomas, UPI White House Bureau chief

1976   Louis Harris, Harris Poll
        Frank Quine, American Press Institute

1977   Judith D. Hines, American Newspaper Publishers Association
            Foundation, Washington, D.C.
        George Nigh, Lieutenant Governor of Oklahoma
        Bill Mullen, executive vice president, National Newspaper Asso-
            ciation

1978   Bob Bullock, Texas Comptroller
        Walton L. Huff, Exxon USA

1979   Chip Babcock, Tom Williams, Jack Balagia, and J. Tullos Wells
        Billy Clayton, Speaker of the Texas House
        Reginald Whitman, CEO, MKT Railroad
        Lieutenant Governor Bill Hobby
        Abe Lemons, basketball coach, University of Texas

1980   Governor Bill Clements
        Earl Campbell, football star, Texan of the Year Award
        Joe B. Frantz, Walter Prescott Webb Professor of History, Univer-
            sity of Texas
        Jack Landau, Reporter's Committee for Freedom of the Press
        U.S. Senator John Tower

1981   Master Sergeant Roy Benavides, Medal of Honor recipient, Texan
            of the Year Award

1982 Garrett Ray, *Littleton (Colo.) Independent*
John M. Lounge, U.S. astronaut
Julian Read, Read Poland Associates
Larry Gatlin, singer, Texan of the Year Award

1983 Ann Richards, State Treasurer of Texas
Lynn Ashby, *Houston Post*

1984 Maureen Santini, chief of AP White House correspondents
J. Kerby Anderson, Probe Ministries, Dallas
U.S. Representative Phil Gramm

1985 T. Boone Pickens Jr., Mesa Petroleum
Paul Burka, *Texas Monthly*
Kent Hance, former U.S. congressman

1986 Lynn Ashby, *Houston Post*
Representative Stan Schleuter, Texas House
First Amendment Panel, Chip Babcock et al.

1987 Paul Burka, *Texas Monthly*
U.S. Senator Lloyd Bentsen

1988 Bob Bullock, Texas Comptroller
Dr. Bernard Weinstein, Center for Enterprising

1989 George W. Bush, owner, Texas Rangers baseball club
Mike Cochran, roving correspondent, Associated Press

1990 Jan Naylor, special assistant to President George H. W. Bush
Tony Pederson, *Houston Chronicle*, photojournalism ethics

1991 Joseph L. Galloway, *U.S. News and World Report*
John Papanek, *Sports Illustrated*
Governor Ann Richards

1992 Chris Matthews, Washington Bureau chief, *San Francisco
Examiner*
Lionel "Skip" Meno, Texas Education Commissioner
Carolyn Warmbold, *San Antonio Light*

1993   Rick Perry, Texas Agriculture Commissioner
       Red McCombs, San Antonio businessman
       Lieutenant Governor Bob Bullock
       Gary Bledsoe, special counsel to the Texas Attorney General

1994   John Roach, president, Tandy Corporation
       Governor Ann Richards
       Gubernatorial candidate George W. Bush
       U.S. Senator Kay Bailey Hutchison

1995   James A. "Andy" Collins, director, Texas Department of Criminal
           Justice
       Representative Layton Black, Texas House

1996   Martha Jean McHaney, *Denver Post*
       Shelburn Wilkes, "All in the First Family"

1997   Pete Laney, Speaker of the Texas House
       John Erickson, author of the *Hank the Cowdog* books

1998   Laura Welch Bush, First Lady of Texas
       Chip Babcock
       Dan Cook, *San Antonio Express-News*
       Bob Danzig, Hearst Newspapers

1999   Lesley Anne Fair, Federal Trade Commission
       Lynne Meena, "The Power of Newsprint"

2000   Dr. Shall Sinha, Gandhi impersonator
       Mike Peters, creator of the *Mother Goose and Grimm* comic strip
       Senator Jeff Wentworth, Texas Senate
       Mitch Henderson, MarketPro International
       Daniel Russ, GSD&M Advertising, Austin

2001   Mary Gordon Spence, humorist
       Steve Murdock, Texas State Data Center, Texas A&M University

2002 Mike Morrow, Windham School District, Texas Department of
Criminal Justice
Bob Scaife, Newspaper Association of America
Ken Bronson, Kansas Press Association
Howard Helmer, American Egg Board
Byron Sage, Federal Bureau of Investigation (retired)
Michelle McLellan, special projects editor, *The Oregonian*
(Portland)

2003 Frank L. Culbertson Jr., former U.S. astronaut
Jock Lauterer, Carolina Media Project
Tony Marsella, Morris Communications

2004 Dave Einsel, *Houston Chronicle*
Lucy Dalglish, Reporter's Committee for Freedom of the Press
Greg Abbott, Texas Attorney General
Tom Squitieri, *USA Today*
Liz Carpenter, former press secretary and chief of staff for
Lady Bird Johnson
Lieutenant Governor David Dewhurst
Admiral James Godwin, U.S. Navy

Texas Winners
of Pulitzer Prizes

Since 1955, Texas journalists and publications have received 19 Pulitzer Prize Awards in Journalism. The Pulitzer Prize Web site has complete lists of Pulitzer Prize winners by year of award.

MERITORIOUS PUBLIC SERVICE

1961—Amarillo Globe-Times, for exposing a breakdown in local law enforcement, resulting in punitive action that swept lax officials from their posts.

1977—Lufkin News, for an obituary of a local man who died in Marine training camp, resulting in an investigation leading to reform in recruiting and training practices of the U.S. Marine Corps.

1985—Fort Worth Star-Telegram (reporter, Mark J. Thompson), for revealing that 250 U.S. servicemen had lost their lives as a result of a design problem in helicopters built by Bell Helicopter.

LOCAL REPORTING

[(1) General/Spot; (2) Special/Investigative]

1955—(1) Mrs. Caro Brown, *Alice Daily Echo*, for her series of news stories dealing with one-man political rule in Duval County.

1955—(2) Roland Kenneth Towery, *Cuero Record*, for his series of articles exposing a scandal in the administration of the Veterans' Land Program in Texas.

SOURCE: *Texas Almanac 2004–2005*

1963—(2) Oscar Griffin Jr., *Pecos Independent and Enterprise*, for his exposure of the Billie Sol Estes scandal.

1965—(2) Gene Goltz, *Houston Post*, for his expose of government corruption in Pasadena, Texas.

1992—(2) Lorraine Adams and Dan Malone, *The Dallas Morning News*, for their series on police abuse of authority.

NATIONAL REPORTING

1986—Craig Flournoy and George Rodrigue, *The Dallas Morning News*, for their investigation into subsidized housing in East Texas, which uncovered patterns of racial discrimination and segregation in public housing across the United States and led to significant reforms.

INTERNATIONAL REPORTING

1994—A team of 30 writers, photographers, artists and editors from *The Dallas Morning News* for a series on violence against women. The team comprised the following:

Writers: Toni Y. Joseph, Joseph Kahn, Gregory Katz, Melanie Lewis, Victoria Loe, Pam Maples, David L. Marcus, Gayle Reaves, Anne Reifenberg and George Rodrigue.

Photographers: Paula Nelson, Karen Stallwood, Beatriz Terrazas, Judy Walgren and Cindy Yamanaka.

Graphics: Don Huff, Marco A. Ruiz and Kathleen Vincent.

Editors: Mary Carter, Ricardo Chavira, Linda Crosson, John Davidson, Patricia Gaston, Kerry Gunnels, Robert Hart, Ed Kohorst, Jim Landers, Lennox Samuels, Sue F. Smith, and Lisa Thatcher.

EXPLANATORY JOURNALISM

1989—David Hanners (reporter), William Snyder (photographer) and Karen Blessen (artist), *The Dallas Morning News*, for their special report on the investigation into a 1985 airplane crash.

PHOTOGRAPHY

1964—Robert H. Jackson, *Dallas Times Herald*, for his photograph of the murder of Lee Harvey Oswald by Jack Ruby.

SPOT NEWS PHOTOGRAPHY

1981—Larry C. Price, *Fort Worth Star-Telegram*, for photographs from Liberia.

1988—Scott Shaw, *Odessa American*, for his photo of Jessica McClure being rescued from a well.

1993—Ken Geiger and William Snyder, *The Dallas Morning News*, for their photos of the 1992 Summer Olympics.

FEATURE PHOTOGRAPHY

1980—Erwin H. Hagler, *Dallas Times Herald*, for a series on the Western cowboy.

1983—James B. Dickman, *Dallas Times Herald*, for his photographs of life and death in El Salvador.

1991—William Snyder, *The Dallas Morning News*, for his photographs of Romanian orphans.

CARTOONS

1982—Ben Sargent, *Austin American-Statesman.*

Ben Sargent © 1981 *Austin American-Statesman.*
Used courtesy of the cartoonist and Universal Press
Syndicate. All rights reserved.